Ministry to the Armed Forces

TABLE OF CONTENTS

Ron Bowman

Ministry to the Armed Forces

INTRODUCTION:

An Immense Opportunity

THE "Ministry to the Armed Forces" begins and ends in the civilian congregation. It is a big ministry. How big? This big:

- Over 36.0 million men between the ages of 18 and 35 are now registered in the Selective Service System.

- 2.5 million young civilian church members turn 18 annually—half of them young men who face a military obligation and must register for the draft.

- In July, 1966 there were 2.8 million persons on active duty in the Armed Forces of the United States. Their average age was twenty. With 3.0 million dependents, they made a total military community of 5.9 million. (Assumed: an all-service average of 1.1 dependents per man in uniform[1]) If the 1968 figure of 3.5 million servicemen is used, the military community becomes 7.3 million.

- Of the 1966 military community 4.5 million were church members.[2] This was 3.5% of the 125,778,656 members claimed in 1966 by 241 religious bodies.

[1] From *Journal of the Armed Forces*. 6/8/68, p. 6.
[2] Based on a U.S. population of 196,842,000 in July, 1966. The church membership claimed is 64 percent of this and is the figure used in computing church membership in the Armed Forces. (cf. *World Almanac*, 1968 Ed. p. 175)

- From their 330,452 congregations these bodies provided the Armed Forces with 4,000 chaplains. Several thousand more are reservists.

- 750,000 persons leave military service each year.

- Thousands of churches located close to military installations have an oportunity to minister to servicemen.

Broad in Scope

Not only does the ministry to the Armed Forces involve large numbers of people. Its scope is far-ranging; in one form or another it touches virtually all the contemporary issues facing our society. It is a further illustration of the fact that the "mission" of religion today is one and can no longer be fragmented into unrelated sectors. As we are so painfully discovering, everything is related to everything else.

In pastoral terms this ministry ranges from pre-active duty instruction and counsel, through active military service, to the resumption of civilian status. It addresses itself to young adult civilians of both sexes, young single men and women in uniform, military families, "waiting wives" and their children, and finally, to those who have completed military service and are rejoining the civilian community. Responsibility for it rests with the churches and cannot be delegated to the chaplains, who are but one expression of it. Military chaplains cannot, for example, counsel civilian young people about the draft. This is a civilian task—too long neglected.

The churches must somehow speak more effectively to young adults. Whether in business or industry, in college or on the farm, in the Armed Forces or unemployed, the young man or woman of eighteen represents an identifiable "youth culture" which by sheer weight of numbers dominates our society. It continues to be true that military service can be a salutary experience for a young man; even the interrupting of a college program to enter the Forces has been termed useful. The pastoral ministry to the young adult is virtually emasculated if it omits the consideration of military service. Equipping clergymen and others to carry out a better ministry in this area should be a major concern of religious leaders at every level.

The Pre-Active Duty phase of this ministry is considered in some detail in chapters 1-6. Briefly, it involves:

1. Stronger programs of religious education, viz.
    a) Inclusion of teaching about privilege and obligation with respect to citizenship in the United States; giving encouragement to the concept of "National Service" in any of its many forms (cf. p. 48).
    b) Offering information about Selective Service and military service in church youth programs, plus instruction about the religious issues these may raise.
2. Pastoral counseling to individuals on these subjects.
3. Public recognition and remembrance in church services of those facing a military obligation. Presentation of prayer books, medals, etc.
4. Full inclusion of conscientious objectors of whatever type within pastoral and congregational concern.

Chapters 7-14 deal with the ministry to those who wear the uniform. Though the major burden of this falls upon the chaplains, there is much that civilian congregations can do to support and supplement their work. In crisis situations chaplain and civilian clerics must often work together. Having "endorsed" chaplains and loaned them to the Government, denominations must steadfastly reassure them that they are held in esteem and give them to know that they are not the forgotten men of the ministry, off in a limbo of their own.

Certain social issues such as alcoholism, narcotics, and homosexuality present themselves within military life also. One issue, racial discrimination, has been sharply reduced, so much so that the Negro's dream of getting a "fair shake" is far more nearly realized in the Armed Forces than in civilian life. The civilians are those who still refuse to rent apartments to Negro servicemen. Military service itself rests in the context of a civilian society; issues of great significance affect it. Some of these are: the responsible use of power in the modern world; the nature of patriotism on a shrinking planet; the internationalizing of military forces under the United Nations; the limiting on every level of the resort to violence; and the continuance of conscription. These bear directly on military service and are in a sense preliminary to it.

Finally, the resettlement of the returning veteran offers the churches still further pastoral opportunities—particularly if the veteran is a Negro. (Cf. Chapter 15.)

4

An Immense Opportunity

All this lies within what we term the "Ministry to the Armed Forces." It is timely, urgent, and full of challenge. The day when it might have been understood mainly as "cake and cookies for our boys" (though these are still welcome!) is long gone. It is a many-faceted concern for people in every city and hamlet who are, or soon will be, in their country's service. It is, moreover, an on-going ministry. In all probability, the size of our Armed Forces will not dip below 2.5 million in the near future. The lowest post-World War II level was 1,398,000, reached in 1948, compared with 334,473 on June 30, 1939 and 3,489,000 on the same date in 1968. We shall continue to have a large military organization requiring the continuance of the draft and large numbers of chaplains. It is not possible to regard ministering to the Armed Forces as primarily a war-time activity. A ministry to a community of over 7,000,000 souls is huge by any standard—and this does not count those additional millions to whom the draft is a daily worry. It simply cannot be shoved aside as a peripheral concern.

Finally, it should be noted that this ministry has important links with the church's urban ministry. In seaports and in metropolitan centers one can always find soldiers and sailors on the streets looking for something to do. They have little money. They are victimized easily. Most of them want wholesome entertainment, interesting things to do, attractive girls to talk to and dance with, and some assurance that they are welcome.

The Ministry to the Armed Forces offers the religious community of the United States an immense opportunity.

5

Chapter 1

The Young Adult

IN a total U.S. population of 196,842,000 in July, 1966, over 61,000,000 were under 18, and over 91,000,000 were 24 or under. These proportions approach those existing when the Declaration of Independence was signed. In 1776 half the colonists were under 18. In 1956 two million youngsters turned eighteen annually; by 1965 this figure was four million. One quarter of the 16 to 24 age group is in college. Enrollment in public degree-granting institutions of higher learning rose from 1,484,000 in 1955 to 3,624,000 in 1965 and will reach 6,315,000 by 1975. The eight Ivy League colleges reported 45,591 applications for 7,688 places for the academic years 1966-67. The nation's land-grant colleges spent $158,637,000 in 1953-54 and $614,944,000 in 1963-64. The estimated value of their physical plants rose from $1.96 billion to $5.39 billion.

At the same time many more young people enter the labor market. In October, 1967 over 11,000,000 people between the ages of 18 and 24 held full-time jobs. Of these, nearly 6,000,000 were young men. Nearly a million others were unemployed and out of school. Because of mounting educational requirements it grows steadily harder for young people to get and hold a job. Unskilled jobs are disappearing rapidly. Education's effect on earning capacity has never been so pronounced.

For the first time, America has an enormous, clearly identifiable youth culture. For the remainder of this century young people will dominate the political and economic affairs of this country. They will accept "colonial status" no longer.[1] What, then, are their outlooks?

No Single Profile is Possible

It is impossible to draw a single inclusive profile of the young person of eighteen today because he has too many faces; there are many profiles, not one. Moreover, youth has an innate capacity for concealment.

6

Youth can be so different from itself, as it moves from role to role, that it still maintains, even in a society devoted to publicity, a great capacity for concealment. This masquerade, and the range of youth, and the pace of change, make it difficult to generalize about the young.[2]

Even apart from this natural secretiveness, the times into which these young people have been catapulted make their situation extraordinarily difficult. "Every major industrial society believes that it has a serious youth problem." [3]

Today's 18-year-old, born in 1950, five years after the close of World War II, had scarcely begun to sit up when the Korean War burst upon the already divided United Nations. He saw daylight in the middle of President Truman's second term; he was a toddler when the nation elected its first Republican President since Hoover. He grew up amid an almost continuous succession of major national and world developments, technological and social. He was not yet three when the first hydrogen bomb was tested at Eniwetok. He was four when the U.S. Supreme Court handed down its historic ruling on the inherent inequality of segregated education.

The struggle for civil rights, with its protests both peaceful and violent, has been part of the scene for as long as he can remember. He has never known a world without television. He has always been on wheels, and the older he grows the faster he seems to go. He was seven when the Sputnik circled the globe in the unheard-of time of ninety minutes. His parents bought him a space suit, and a new word was added to his vocabulary. "Astronaut" John Glenn became his hero. N.A.S.A.'s rockets summoned him to the moon and beyond. Musically, he responded wildly to the Beatles. The guitar became the badge of his culture.

He was ten when John F. Kennedy won the Presidency by a bare 119,000 votes, twelve when the missile crisis of 1962 took the country to the brink of war, and thirteen—old enough to remember it well—when its 35th President was assassinated. He has grown up through the cold war, the death of Stalin, the rise and fall of Mr. Khrushchev, and the arrival of the Soviet Union at a more placid stage of development. Communism neither frightens nor excites him. He has never known a major depression. His parents' income has doubled during his lifetime. His up-bringing and education cost more and take longer than ever. He and his peers have ten billion dollars a year to spend, a fact of which the rest of the economy is acutely conscious.

In his lifetime the computer has appeared; data processing machinery has created both revolutionary new possibilities and a need for higher levels of education. The automation of industrial processes has leaped forward. The chances that he will go to college are much greater—as are the odds that he won't finish. That college education, the need for which exercises such a tyranny over him, represents an enormous national enterprise involving the expenditure of 16.8 billion dollars in 1966, up 12.7 billion from 1956.

His years have seen a steady crumbling of barriers between people, both nationally and internationally. He senses a bond with his fellows around the world; the notion of world citizenship attracts him; instinctively, he feels himself beyond an anachronistic nationalism. He is cosmopolitan and urbanized, a child of the city, a breather of its smog, a contributor to its congestion—and its trash. His parents may have fled to the suburbs—or they may have tried and been turned back.

"Instant everything" is offered him by day and by night. The "commercial" has bred in him a thorough-going skepticism, yet he is seldom without his little transistor radio. The Dollar, the Job, Status, Leisure, and Sex are hawked on every side. He has arrived at the age of experimentation just at the time when the Pill has made the sexual relationship less risky. Beyond this beckons the intriguing, if dangerous, world of narcotics. Beside such possibilities, alcohol seems "kid stuff."

The Peace Corps, with its demand for sacrifice, attracts him, but he is skeptical about Mr. Johnson's Great Society. He was a high school freshman when the bitter election of 1964 divided the land. Since that time the name "Vietnam" has sounded ever more ominously in his ears. Associated with it is a clumsy draft which may thrust him into mortal combat with an enemy he doesn't know or hate. He has witnessed the rise of violence in America. His protests and counter-protests spread across the land. Moods of alienation, apathy, and despair drain away much of his creativity.

Such is the world in which the eighteen-year-old finds himself in 1968. It creates his present and also the possibilities from which he must build his future. He understands, probably better than his elders, that change will remain a permanent and an accelerating phenomenon in his life. He is more open to social change than are his parents. "New conceptions of the family, of the relations between the sexes, of work, residence, leisure, of the role of government, and the place of

America in world affairs" [4] are the accustomed fabric of his thought. He is in society, but not yet fully of it. He feels its effects, yet can stand apart from it. He is able to evaluate it with an objectivity, accuracy, and candor which can disconcert the most sympathetic adult. What he sees does not reassure him. He finds much to criticize in the world his elders open to him, yet he has no great sureness within himself about what he would build in its place. He seeks commitment, but not yet . . .

HIS RESPONSES IN THE LIGHT OF HIS NEEDS

1. Resignation to Delay

To assume his place as an adult, a young person must become equipped to earn his living. This takes more and more time. A high school diploma no longer represents a sufficient level of education for successful entrance into modern computerized, automated industry. A college degree, or at least some years of post-high school study, are required. Over 800,000 young people are enrolled in two-year colleges.

This need for educational preparation and its growing difficulty in terms of content, duration, and cost is a source of frustration to the energetic, physically-matured, independence-minded young person. It spells a lengthened dependency, delay in marriage or, as more frequently happens, earlier marriage, and acceptance of support by parents, in-laws, and wife. On the opposite side of this coin and more ominous for the future is the hopelessness of those for whom no such preparation is possible. Theirs will be the bitter frustration of knowing that "a technical society has no use for a pool of unskilled labor," [5] a frustration certain to explode if it goes unrelieved.

2. Retreat into His Own Culture

American society is compartmentalized. At one end of the time scale are the elderly and at the other, in a culture all their own, are the young. Theirs is a culture within a culture with values of its own which emphasize "disengagement from adult values, sexual attractiveness, daring immediate pleasure and comradeship in a way that is true neither of childhood nor of adulthood. The youth culture is not always or explicitly anti-adult, but it is belligerently non-adult." [6] It serves as a sanctuary within which it is possible for the moment to postpone adulthood while continuing the search for a solid identity and for the meaningful commitments which are the essence of adult-hood. The outstanding characteristics of those within this culture are "their great numbers, their homogeneity, prosperity, their prolonged dependency, socialization, and education." [7] Of all the nations on earth the United States "has the longest experience with the subculture of youth as it develops in a modern society." [8]

Exposure to a much wider experience of life at an earlier age reinforces youth's native instinct to withdraw. Young people possess a level of sophistication which sets them apart from their elders and makes communicating with them more difficult. The huge and continuing expansion of public higher education generates collegiate values and styles of life among all the young, and this only widens the generational gap.

The very rapid increase in the younger educated groups has recently widened the gap between the 15-year-old and the 50-year-old in our society. They label as cynical a youthful response to mass media that is based on skills they do not possess. The fact that the most popular visiting place for servicemen in New York, after the Empire State Building, is the Museum of Modern Art suggests that young people are participants in a cosmopolitan culture from which most older members of the society, because of provincialism and lack of training, are excluded.[9]

Even high schoolers behave like collegians—and resemble them more closely than was true thirty years ago.

3. Studied Indifference

The finding of values and setting of goals is central among the preparatory tasks of youth. This too, is more difficult than it used to be. One must not hastily fault the young for their seeming "lack of deep commitments to adult values and roles." [10] They see the adult world as "a cold, mechanical, abstract, specialized, and emotionally meaningless place in which one simply goes through the motions, but without conviction that the motions are worthy, humane, dignified, relevant, or exciting. Thus . . . it is essential to stay 'cool'; and 'coolness' involves detachment, lack of commitment, never being enthusiastic, or going overboard about anything." [11] Adults need to understand that this posture at least makes it possible to avoid "damaging commitment to false life styles and goals." [12] The young are acutely observant and shrewd.

10

—the sanity of young people today is partly manifest in their awareness that their world is very different from that of their parents. They know that rash commitments may prove outmoded tomorrow; they know that most viewpoints are rapidly shifting; they therefore find it difficult to locate a fixed position on which to stand.[13]

Kenniston's gloomy assertion that "parents are increasingly irrelevant as models for their children"[14] does not hold for the early, "formative" years. The eighteen-year-old is the product of parental molding.

Attitudes and behavior of eighteen-year-olds are controlled to a considerable degree by an internal gyroscope which was formed and set during the years before ten, and their actions should not be judged without knowledge of this mechanism and the extent of its effect.[15]

With this proviso one can accept Kenniston's remark that "the very sanity and realism" of young people sometimes leads them to be disaffected from the values of their elders.[16] Theirs is a different situation, and time does "make ancient good uncouth."

Parents are, as Blaine maintains, still obligated—and able—to offer their youngsters good models, objective information at many, if not all, points and a strong personal challenge for the future.[17] The affectation of neutrality that often masks adult uncertainty and lack of commitment is precisely what young people despise in their elders. All too correctly do they surmise that others also are groping.

4. Open to Vital Religion

Behind their facade of detachment young people are busy seeking values by which to live. They will respond to vital ideals from the past if these are attractively and compellingly advanced. They are open to the influence of religion.[18] At the same time, however, they seek new ideals, new values, new goals which will be relevant and useful in the world that is coming.

It is for such ideals that young people are searching: they need foundations for their lives which will link them to their personal and communal pasts and to their present society but which at the same time will provide a trustworthy basis for their futures. The total emulation or total rejection of the older generation by the young must be replaced by a recreation in each generation of the living and relevant aspects of the past, and by the creation of new images of life which will provide points of constancy in a time of rapid change.[19]

As they pick their way into the wilderness of the future, young people need patience, honesty, and firmness from adults. It is harder than it ever was to come into a man's estate.

NOTES

1. "Adolescents are among the last social groups in the world to be given the full nineteenth-century colonial treatment." *Coming of Age in America: Growth and Acquiescence* by Edgar Z. Friedenberg, Vintage Books, 1963 (300 pp.) $1.95 (paper) pp. 4 ff.
2. Ruel Denney's essay, "American Youth Today" in *Youth: Change and Challenge* edited by Erik H. Erikson, Basic Books, 1961, p. 138
3. Friedenberg, *op. cit.* p. 3
4. Kenneth Kenniston's essay, "Social Change and Youth in America," Erikson, *op. cit.* p. 166
5. Friedenberg, *op. cit.* p. 7
6. Kenniston, *op. cit.* p. 177
7. Denney, *op. cit.* p. 132
8. *Ibid.* p. 131
9. *Ibid.* pp. 139-40
10. Kenniston, *op. cit.* p. 170
11. *Ibid.*
12. *Ibid.* p. 171
13. *Ibid.*
14. *Ibid.*
15. *Youth and the Hazards of Affluence, the High School and College Years* by Graham B. Blaine, M.D., N.Y. Harper & Row, 1966, p. 3
16. Kenniston, *op. cit.* pp. 171 ff.
17. Blaine, *op. cit.* pp. 128 ff.
18. *Ibid., op. cit.* pp. 114 ff.
19. Kenniston, *op. cit.* p. 186
The above books contain extensive bibliographies.

Chapter 2

The Counseling Task

I N A RAPIDLY changing, technological, urbanized, pressure-packed society it is critically important that wise counsel be readily available to young people.

The question is not whether there should be guidance, but who should give it, how much effort should go into it, and how it can be improved.[1] While this need is not new, its urgency has been underscored recently by its absence in a particular context—that of the military obligation. The Military Selective Service Act of 1967 lays upon each American male between the ages of 18 and 35 a military obligation whose fulfillment, possible in many ways, requires thought and planning. Military service is one of the major, but by no means useless, intrusions into one's private life. Yet, with adequate counsel and planning, it need not be a disruption.[2] The eighteen-year-old is on the threshold of change. The summons to military service brings crisis upon him—the more severe because it takes him by surprise. The possibility of his being drafted seems remote up to and sometimes beyond his eighteenth birthday. The issues of military service are not "live." An "it can't happen to me" attitude builds up and is not dispelled. Suddenly what "couldn't happen" happens. His unpreparedness increases his agitation and confusion. Questions of fact about Selective Service and alternative possibilities suddenly become important— and immediate.

A Neglected Task

Few secondary schools, public or private, offer serious instruction about military service or the draft. Many simply turn an assembly over to a recruiter once a year. In retrospect, this seems odd, since military service presents a significant opportunity to develop and grow in health, education, social skills and perspectives, and maturity. Professor Ginzberg asserts that counsel in regard to military service is one of the four major areas in which guidance is most pertinent to a young person.[3]

13

Still fewer are the churches which offer young people factual information and mature guidance about the obligation to serve one's country, about the draft, and the Armed Forces. Some clergymen now question the morality of military service and of a draft to provide manpower for an unpopular war. Their protests dramatize the need for what they themselves have hitherto almost totally neglected. Churchmen have missed an important task, one which will need attention for years to come. The global involvements of the United States will require a large military force for the foreseeable future. However much the 1967 Statute may need improvement,[4] the draft remains a hard reality for young men—and hence for their parents, sweethearts, and brides. All may turn to the clergyman for counsel.

The church has some time-tested observations about the occasion for and circumstances of military service. The central question about the killing of another human being, or of many, is but the most critical of several pertinent topics with which the church has had long experience. It has something to say, for example, about the redemption of time. It might well suggest to young people that a tour in the Armed Forces need not be "two years of my life gone down the drain."[5]

The Counselor's Aims and Qualifications

School guidance personnel, clergymen in parishes and on college campuses, laymen and women, and military recruiters bear the burden of the counseling task. Local draft boards have an officially appointed Advisor to Registrants.[6]

There are three crucial qualifications for effective counseling: (1) a sympathetic interest in the person who comes; (2) the possession of or access to needed information; and (3) the ability to remain reasonably objective. Other skills and training may perhaps be needed, but these three are essential, particularly in connection with young people. Sympathetic interest comes first. The counselor of the young must like, if not understand, them. He must appreciate the pressures under which they live and realize how difficult it can be to find one's self. "Patience and fortitude" will be important assets, and, when a measure of maturity, some common sense, and a willingness to listen are added, the troubled youngster may decide that a friend is at hand. "Maturity" implies the possession of a broad experience with life and some ability at self-discipline. If the counselor's background includes military service, he is usually, though not infallibly, ahead of the game. The veteran may have to remind himself that the world facing today's

14

young people is not that of pre-atomic bomb, pre-jet, pre-television, Hitlerite 1941, and that military service is also radically different, at least in its technical aspects. In other respects it has not altered; it still contains regimentation, drill, testing, boredom, danger, and the ancient perils awaiting the soldier on liberty. However, its opportunities are also greater.

About these and other matters the counselor must be prepared to "level" with the young person in his study. The youthful "client" will be perceptive and will have a sharp eye for affectation—and a still sharper aversion to it. Evasion will be fatal to the relationship. Yet, "leveling" is not "solving." The young man will resent any attempt to solve his problem for him. He both wants and needs to do it himself. The counselor's task is to help him help himself.

Chapter One cites some of the many excellent books about today's young people. The present chapter lists some books on pastoral counseling.[7] As he accumulates experience the counselor will discover the sources of needed information. Many are supplied in this volume.

Polarization Is All Too Easy

Objectivity in pre-military counseling is vitally important—and easily lost. Military service raises sensitive religious and ethical issues, the subjects of deeply held convictions. Yet, whether he be pacifist or participationist, the counselor must not attempt to persuade his counselee of the merits of his personal position. Any such attempt will be resented. It will frustrate the young person and short-circuit the counseling relationship. This cannot be stressed too strongly.

On no issues do people polarize more quickly than those of war and peace. The crisis now triggering this reaction is the American involvement in Vietnam. To avoid polarization and the attendant blindness to other points of view is extraordinarily difficult—but possible. For the counselor it is essential. A tight rein on personal viewpoints will enable him to serve the interests of his "client," his congregation, and his community—all of whom have a stake in what he says and does.

What the Counselor Faces

The young man may arrive in a black mood, with a bagful of mixed feelings.

. . . most young men grow up without any understanding of military

15

obligation, with the consequence that if and when they are called to duty, they view it as an imposition, an annoyance, or a stroke of bad luck that they were caught while so many others escaped.[8]

Apprehension, idealism, resentment, anger, bitterness, frustration, cynicism, fatalism, and rebelliousness may chase each other around without him, each suggesting its own precipitate course of action. His hostility to "establishments," including those of the church, may be pronounced. The uncertainty stemming from his inability to make firm plans may gnaw at his innards. He may appear shortly before his eighteenth birthday to discuss his impending registration. Or, he may come as a crestfallen student whose declining grades mean dropping out of school and losing his deferment.

Citizens in all walks of life are rightly disturbed about the alienation of the young from society today.

For a democracy to permit and encourage its young men to grow up viewing military service as a burden to be avoided is an invitation to national disaster.[9]

But students comprise only a small portion of the manpower pool—2.5 million out of over 20 million.[10] The counselor may see more young men from business and industry—or without jobs. The requirement that their jobs be kept open for them may be only token compensation; on the other hand, the military interruption may prove providential.

A study in depression, the draft reject may come to the counselor. Possibilities for "rehabilitation," some of them Service-conducted, will need exploration. It is not pleasant to be told "Your country has no use for you."

Counseling the "Conscientious Participant"

The young man may come with his course of action fully charted and may wish merely to test it on a respected listener. If he plans to enter the service, the counselor's task, though simpler, does not vanish. His job now is to alert the youngster to some things which lie ahead and to support him in his decision. The trauma of basic training should be discussed, along with the fact that the young man will feel rage, frustration, and revolt at first—will want to talk back and complain of the "rough" tactics, hate his drill instructor, and despise the tasks given him as beastly or stupid. If he knows he'll face these emotions

16

and that they will be shared by everyone with him, he can better accept them. If he knows that later they will change into feelings of pride in his ability to do any task, however menial or complex, his transition will be eased.

The counselor need not dwell overlong on drinking, women, gambling, and swearing. While not unimportant, these are obvious, and the young man has heard much about them already. He can be given encouraging words on handling loneliness, boredom, fear, temptations, and foreign travel. Loneliness particularly is a great problem. A youngster can play just so many games of ping pong, see just so many movies, eat at a civilian restaurant just so many times, and then loneliness sets in. Some of the training camps are in isolated areas in which the civilian communities are inundated by servicemen on liberty.

Counseling should make the young man aware of all this and suggest wholesome solutions: good companions, sports, the hobby shops, and correspondence courses. Contacts with fine girls are often difficult in a small town or a community in which he spends only a short time, but they are possible. Most churches have young peoples' clubs which welcome servicemen. The various poverty programs are anxious to have off-duty volunteers help with tutoring, being a big brother, etc. The young man's resolve to make the most of his service years should certainly be supported; the man who comes sullenly into service will create problems for himself and for others.

The serviceman will meet his unit chaplain upon arrival at his permanent duty station. His home pastor can provide him with a letter of introduction to the clergy and people of his denomination wherever he goes. He can write to the chaplain to tell him of his parishioner's coming. The young man can be alerted to the ecumenical encounters in military life—and to the likelihood of his being led in worship by a pastor not of his own denomination. A clergyman can present a young man with a prayer book, medal, or other token of the congregation's interest. Pre-service counsel is but the initial expression of this interest. Even more important is the writing of letters. Servicemen whom the church has remembered during an absence will not return home with the embittered conviction that church people "couldn't care less."

In these various ways the pre-service counselor can lay the foundation for a rewarding and continuing relationship with his young adults.

Counseling the "Conscientious Objector"

When a young man announces that he cannot in conscience participate in military service, a different situation arises, and the counselor will behave accordingly. A fuller discussion of this appears in Chapter Six. Here it should be stressed (1) that the counselor must respect the young objector, protect his integrity, make certain that he understands what he is doing and why, the probable consequences, alternative service possibilities, and the steps to be taken. Should the young man remain firm, the counselor must be prepared to stay with him as a true pastor and friend and, within the limits of his ability and resources, see him through the experience; and (2) that his long-term obligation to his congregation and to society legally prohibits his advocacy of deliberate law-breaking. It is a federal crime to counsel evasion of the Selective Service law. Draft counseling ought not to be an occasion for encouraging civil disobedience. It does indeed mean seeing that a Registrant knows his rights under the law and helping him to assert them. This is precisely the function of the familiar income tax counselor. Neither the tax nor the draft counselor, however, may legally instruct in the evading of the respective obligations. Both abet, within the limits of the law, the resisting of the obligation and the minimizing of its cost. But there are limits!

Remember the Ladies!

Any outline of pre-service counseling which failed to include women would be seriously incomplete. The eighteen-year-old girl is as much a citizen as her draft-eligible brother. In some countries she is drafted! All that affects her country affects her. She has her own convictions and eventually will vote. She can also enlist in the Armed Forces. They offer her opportunities for education, travel, interesting work, and the chance to meet many potential husbands. Nurses are particularly needed, and training scholarships are available. Over 35,000 women are now in uniform.

For the girl who never enters the service there is every likelihood that her fiancé or husband will. She may have to decide whether to hasten or defer marriage to a young serviceman. As a soldier's bride she will join a vast company of women for whom life can be both miserably difficult and deeply satisfying. In her loneliness, she will tend small children, keep things going, and await her husband's return. Marriage and Military Service is discussed more fully in Chapter Thirteen.

Group Counseling

The Vietnam issue has greatly stimulated draft counseling activity, and much experimentation is underway. The National Council of Churches and several denominational assemblies have supported these efforts. The American Friends Service Committee has established a draft counselor training program. Some helpful material has been published.[11]

The simplest type of counseling is the one-to-one relationship. In the area of our concern this has two disadvantages, (1) the crisis atmosphere which usually surrounds it, and (2) the fact that many young men never appear at the clergyman's door. Group counseling meets both of these objections. It can be planned more carefully; it can include various age levels and both sexes. The sharing of common problems and frank discussion of sensitive issues become possible. A good deal more can be accomplished.

Finally, draft counseling is a significant opportunity for joint action across denominational lines. The establishment by a group of churches of a Draft Counseling Center can be a great contribution to a community. Such a facility must be open to all, operate lawfully, and try sincerely to deal objectively and honestly with every pastoral situation, every shade of opinion presented it.

NOTES

1. *The Optimistic Tradition and American Youth* by Eli Ginzberg et al. Columbia University Press, 1962, p. 113.
2. For some positive aspects of dropping out of school temporarily, cf. *Youth and the Hazards of Affluence, op. cit.* pp. 33-6 (cf. p. 16 this volume).
3. Ginzberg, *op. cit.* p. 115.
4. Ginzberg, *op. cit.* pp. 78-81; also pp. 39-40 of this volume.
5. Ginzberg, *op. cit.* pp. 81-3.
6. In its notable report the Marshall Commission says that "appeal agents are almost totally inactive." (p. 28) cf. pp. 39-40 of this volume.
7. *Basic Types of Pastoral Counseling* by Howard J. Clinebell, Jr., N.Y. Abingdon-Cokesbury, 1966.
   Principles and Practices of Pastoral Care by Russell Dicks, Prentice-Hall, 1963, 136 pp. $3.95.
   Pastoral Counseling by Seward Hiltner, Abingdon-Cokesbury, 1949, 291 pp.
8. Ginzberg, *op. cit.* p. 85.
9. Ginzberg, *op. cit.* p. 86.

10. *Selective Service,* July, 1968; bulletin of SSS.
11. *Draft Counseling and Education Centers,* AFSC booklet, 20 pp. free. Order from AFSC, 160 N. 15th St., Philadelphia, Pa. 19102.
1968-1969 Youth Ministry Notebook, a joint publication of four denominations. N.Y. Seabury Press, 1968, 109 pp. $3.00. Part II, pp. 22-45 is particularly good; lists books & films; describes several draft conferences, discusses issues fully; many suggestions.
Episcopal Young Churchmen's Notebook, 1966-1967; "War: Dilemma for Christians," pp. 56-76; Excellent study guide. N.Y. Seabury Press, $3.00.

20

Chapter 3

Educational Opportunities in the Armed Forces

XCEPT during general war, the Armed Forces as a whole can be considered as one huge training and educational enterprise." Consider:

• An estimated 883,000 recruits will enter basic training in fiscal year 1969. This is over 240,000 more men than entered all the colleges of the United States in 1966. About 750,000 men leave the Armed Forces annually. Replacements must be procured and trained.

• "Relatively few enlisted personnel in the Armed Forces are assigned to purely combat specialties. The vast majority of enlisted men work in technical, administrative, and clerical areas, and at the higher skill levels—all of which require a considerable amount of formal training. . . . It is also obvious . . . that the Armed Forces have very little need for the unskilled."

• At any given moment approximately 20 percent of all Armed Forces personnel are "either in formal training programs or occupy assignments in support of these programs. In 1968 the cost of these programs will be 4.3 billion dollars." In 1966 this expenditure amounted to 3.091 billion, or ten percent of the total U.S. annual expenditure for all education, elementary, secondary, and collegiate.

• The five services maintain approximately 300 specialized schools for enlisted personnel. Together these offer more than 2,000 separate courses and, in the fiscal year 1963 graduated over 370,000 students at a cost of just over one billion dollars. Courses vary in length from a few days to as long as forty-two weeks; students are in the classroom or laboratory a full six to eight hours daily.

• Five service academies enroll approximately 17,000 men and cost about $137,000,000 per year to operate. Over 2,500 will be graduated annually.

• The Department of Defense supports 499 ROTC units in U.S. colleges. In fiscal 1968 and 1969 thirty more units will be established.

By 1969 263,000 students will be in the ROTC program and 23,000 will be commissioned annually.

- Officers Candidate Schools will graduate 34,000 new officers in 1968.
- More than 1,000,000 servicemen are enrolled in the 1,700 correspondence courses offered by the combined services. In addition civilian high school, vocational, and college correspondence courses are available at little or no cost through the U.S. Armed Forces Institute at Madison, Wisconsin.
- In September, 1964 the Defense Department operated 23 schools in the U.S. for children of servicemen. Located in areas where the local community failed to provide "suitable free public education," these schools were staffed by 1,742 teachers and contained 38,282 children.
- In December, 1963 there were 291 service-operated schools for dependents of servicemen stationed with their families overseas. Approximately 155,000 children were attending them and being taught by 6,000 civilian teachers in 28 countries.
- The Department of Defense employs over one million civilians and, under the Government Employees Training Act of 1958, offers them extensive training.
- "By law the Armed Forces must train the recruit for a minimum of four months before he can be assigned to overseas duty."
- From the beginning to the end of his tour the serviceman is subject to almost continuous testing and evaluation. There is no release from this process; promotions are made largely on the basis of his test performance.
- Dependents of Armed Forces personnel stationed overseas may take a wide variety of Government-sponsored courses.
- More and more, the Department of Defense is accepting a role as a rehabilitation agency. Between October, 1967 and September, 1968, 100,000 men, formerly disqualified because of educational deficiencies or correctable physical defects, will be qualified by specially prepared pre-basic training programs and then accepted. "Project 100,000" is the name by which this program is known.
- The GI bill makes it possible for thousands of men to further their education after military service—an indirect, yet powerful stimulus to U.S. education by the Armed Forces.
- Some 200 colleges offer one or more university extension and adult education programs.

"Viewed in almost any way, the Department of Defense and its component parts are more heavily involved in the educational process than any other department or agency of the government."

Sources of Information

Each of the services publishes pamphlets, booklets, and catalogues on current personnel requirements and training programs. Some are expressly for guidance counselors. All can be obtained at local recruiting offices (listed in telephone directories under "U.S. Government") or by writing to the following:

The Adjutant General
Department of the Army
Washington, D.C.   20305

Chief of Naval Personnel
Department of the Navy
(Attn: Director of Recruiting)
Washington, D.C.   20370

Commander
U.S. Air Force Recruiting Service
Randolph Air Force Base,
Texas   78148

Commandant, U.S. Marine
Corps (Code DPO)
Headquarters, Marine Corps
Washington, D.C.   20380

Commandant (PTP-2)
U.S. Coast Guard
Washington, D.C.   20591

Defense Advisory Committee on
Women in the Services
OASD (MP & R), Pentagon
Washington, D.C.   20301

Recruiting personnel are happy to assist clergy and school guidance staffs. They can also supply 16mm sound films, many in color, about life in the Armed Forces. Some of these are listed in the Bibliography. Military film libraries are extensive. Catalogues are available through recruiting offices or various service headquarters.

All branches of the Armed Forces urge young people to complete their high school education and then to go to college if possible. Recruiters tell young people over and over again, "Stay in school! Get that diploma!"

Guaranteed Assignment

Subject to the availability of openings and the ever-present factor of the "needs of the service," enlistees may choose their own specialty field and service school. They must, of course, meet all requirements. To avoid misunderstandings, candidates should check carefully with the recruiter about "guaranteed assignment."

COMMISSIONING PROGRAMS

The Federal Academies

All the academies offer four years of college education leading to a bachelor of science degree. With the exception of the Merchant Marine Academy cadet-midshipmen, graduates receive regular commissions and must serve on active duty for at least five years. Merchant Marine Academy graduates must sail for at least three years in the Merchant Marine.

For admission to any of the five academies a man must: be 17 years (but not over 22 as of 1 July of the year he is admitted), a U.S. citizen of good moral character, and be physically and academically qualified. Academic qualification is determined by College Entrance Examination Board tests. Several types of academy appointments are available.

Young men interested in securing an appointment to one of the academies—other than the Coast Guard Academy—should write to their Senators and Representatives in Congress, or to the academy of their choice. Application should be made in the spring preceding the year in which an appointment is sought. Full particulars concerning the academies can be obtained by writing to:

Director of Admissions and Registrar
United States Military Academy
West Point, N.Y.   10996

Director of Admissions
U.S. Coast Guard Academy
New London, Conn.   06320

Chief of Naval Personnel
Navy Department
Washington, D.C.   20370

The Registrar
U.S. Air Force Academy
Colorado   80840

Dean of Admissions
U.S. Naval Academy
Annapolis, Md.   21402

Admissions Office
U.S. Merchant Marine Academy
Kings Point, N.Y.   11024

ROTC Programs

The ROTC consists of 499 units—Army, Navy, and Air Force—at over 300 public and private colleges and universities throughout the country. ROTC training consists of from three to five hours of military instruction per week and some summer training periods. Advanced ROTC training during junior and senior college years is optional, except under the Navy programs, and students must qualify for admission to an advanced course. ROTC graduates fulfill their military obligation by serving on active duty for stipulated periods of time, ranging from two to five years. The various programs include:

Army ROTC—Programs conducted at 270 colleges and universities in the 50 states and Puerto Rico in both four-year and two-year plans.
Navy ROTC—The Navy Regular ROTC offers 4 years of subsidized education at 54 colleges and universities, and includes Marine Corps.
Air Force ROTC—Is available at 175 schools in 47 states. Has both two and four-year programs.

Complete information about the ROTC programs can be obtained by writing to:

Army ROTC
Fort Monroe, Va.   23351

Chief of Naval Personnel
Navy Department
Washington, D.C.   20370

Commandant, Air Force ROTC
Maxwell Air Force Base
Alabama   36112

Commandant of the Marine Corps
Headquarters, U.S. Marine Corps
Washington, D.C.   20380

Officer Candidate School

College graduates can earn commissions in the Army, Navy, Air Force, Marine Corps, or Coast Guard even though they have had no ROTC or other prior military training. Applications may be made for enlistment from civilian life to attend officer candidate or training schools. Recruiting offices are in all major cities and towns. They will have full information about openings and requirements.

In professional fields such as medicine, nursing, law, and the ministry direct appointments to commissions are available. Programs providing financial assistance to students in law and certain health fields are offered. There are also chaplaincy programs for seminarians (cf. p. 71).

Flight training is available to commissioned officers in each of the Armed Forces who can meet professional and physical requirements and are within prescribed age limits. Concerted effort is being made to increase minority recruiting in all officer programs. Recruiting offices will have full information.

Other College Programs

Servicemen may also study in a variety of university extension and adult education programs. Perhaps the best-known of these is the undergraduate educational program of the University of Maryland. This is available at 196 military installations around the world.

SUMMARY OF OFFICER PROGRAMS
FOR COLLEGE STUDENTS

Service	Ages Eligible	Active Duty After Receipt of Commission	
Navy and Marine Corps	17-21	4 years	NROTC (Regular) provides four years of tuition paid college education, including courses in Naval Science.
	17-21	3 years	NROTC (Contract) provides Naval Science studies in connection with regular college program.
Air Force	14-22	4 years	AFROTC is offered at more than 175 institutions as a two or four-year course of instruction. Limited number of scholarships are available for students in the four-year program. Flight instruction is offered to potential pilots by most units. Graduates desiring flying duties must serve four years after award of aeronautical rating.
Army	14-28	2 years	ROTC offers military training leading to a commission at 270 institutions, and aviation training at 151, along with the regular curriculum. Two and four-year scholarships are available. Aviation graduates will have a three-year active duty obligation.
Marine Corps	17-27	3 years	Platoon Leaders' Class (PLC) provides for participation in two six-week summer training sessions with no training during school term. Aviation officers must serve 3½ years after completion of flight training.
Navy	17-27½	3 years	Reserve Officer Candidate (ROC) program provides for participation in two nine-week summer training sessions and regular evening or weekend drills with a reserve unit during the school year.

	17-26½ (pilot) 17-27½ (non-pilot)	3½ years	Aviation Reserve Officer Candidate (AVROC) Program (pilot and non-pilot) is open to men while they attend college. Upon completion of college they are ordered to flight (pilot) or Flight Officer (non-pilot) training.
Navy	19-27½	3 years	Available to College Graduates: Each of the five armed services offers an intensive school program through which college graduates can become officers. These schools range from 10 to 23 weeks in length. All of them lead to commissions in the Reserve. Coast Guard OCS applicants can be guaranteed aviation training providing they meet the qualifications.
Air Force	20½-29½	4 years	
Army	18-27	2 years	
Marine Corps	20-27	3 years	
Coast Guard	21-26	3 years	

Off-Duty Education

Launched in April, 1942, the United States Armed Forces Institute* enables servicemen to continue their education while on active duty. It offers over two hundred high school, college, and technical vocational correspondence and group study courses, including courses in twenty-four languages. Forty-three colleges and universities work together in offering courses. In 1963, 120,558 new students enrolled in the Institute's correspondence courses, 178,885 in its group study courses, and 13,902 in the correspondence courses of participating colleges—a total of 313,345 new students. The Institute has an elaborate testing program. In a single year it scored 769,647 individual tests, and processed 2.8 million pieces of mail. All USAFI courses are evaluated by the Commission on Accreditation of Service Experiences of the American Council on Education. While the Institute does not grant degrees, colleges do grant degree credits for USAFI work. The determination is made by the college. The cost to the serviceman of USAFI courses is minimal.

BIBLIOGRAPHY

Education in the Armed Forces by James C. Shelburne and Kenneth J Groves, N.Y. The Center for Applied Research in Education, Inc. 1965 (Quotations in the text are from this book)
* Cf. Publications of U.S. Armed Forces Institute, Madison, Wisc. 53703

Chapter 4

Routes into Military Service: Voluntary

OUTSIDE every Post Office and municipal building across America one sees the colorful posters which announce the presence of a military recruiting station. Though not called upon to supplant these experts, those who counsel young men and women do need accurate information about Armed Forces opportunities. The material which follows is from *The High School News Service Report* of September 1967, an official publication of the Department of Defense. It provides a comprehensive summary of the numerous enlistment routes into military service, including opportunities for women. A copy should be in the young adult library of every church.[1] The material in the *Report* describes current requirements and provides a framework within which the counselor can evaluate possibilities with each young person who comes to him. It will always be necessary, however, to go to the recruiting station for authoritative current information.

ENLISTMENT PROGRAMS

Enlistment procedures for all branches of the Armed Forces are similar. There are minor exceptions. Programs differ in length of enlistment and in the opportunity to select specific training and assignment.

Each service has its own recruiters to interview prospective enlistees. Following the initial interview, a general-knowledge type qualification test is given. A birth certificate, Social Security card, and draft card (if registered with Selective Service) will be needed.

After the individual's background data are checked and all other

---

[1] For a copy of the current *Report* and for other helpful material, write High School News Service, Department of Defense, Great Lakes, Illinois 60088. (no charge)

requirements met, he is sent, at Government expense, to an Armed Forces examining and entrance station. There he must pass a rigid physical examination and the Armed Forces Qualification Test (AFQT). With these successfully passed, the applicant is formally enlisted and sent to a recruit training center where his military career begins.

The types of duty and the areas overseas and within the United States to which a serviceman may be assigned depend upon (1) the needs of his service, (2) qualifications, (3) the mission of his service, (4) the international situation, and (5) his personal wishes. Tours of duty range from one year (without dependents) to three years (with dependents).

RESERVE COMPONENTS

Under current Federal law, every young man reaching the age of 18 has a six-year military obligation, including a period of active duty (or active duty for training) and a period in the reserves. This obligation can be met in any of several ways. Enlisting in the regular Armed Forces is one. Another is enlisting in an organized reserve program.

A young man without prior military service can enlist in a reserve program until he receives his Selective Service pre-induction notice. Application for enlistment can be made with any local organized reserve unit of the Army, Navy, Air Force, Marine Corps, or Coast Guard, as well as the Army National Guard and the Air National Guard. Applicants aged 17 to 18½ will receive priority.

All reserve programs involve active duty for training. Normally, this consists of recruit training and basic technical schooling or on-the-job training in a military specialty or occupation. Upon completion of his active duty for training, the reservist returns to the local unit in which he enlisted and serves with it until he has fulfilled the terms of his enlistment.

Reservists in organized units are required to attend training sessions or drills regularly throughout the year, and must spend two weeks annually training in the field. All Army Component paid drill units are required to conduct at least 48 training assemblies a year. These are held evenings, or on weekends, or a combination of both. The annual two-week training period is normally scheduled during the summer.

A reservist is paid for attending two weeks of active duty for training each year. His pay is based on the Armed Forces pay scale for his grade and length of service. He also receives one day's pay for each drill attended. Added to this is full pay for the two weeks of summer field training. He also earns retirement credits. The following table summarizes enlistment, reserve, and aviation programs. Commissioned officer programs are described on pages 24, 25.

SUMMARY: ENLISTED PROGRAMS

I. REGULAR

Service	Ages	Active Duty	
Coast Guard	17-26	4 years	Enlistees may have only one dependent. Specially qualified personnel are selected for specialist training schools immediately following recruit training. Top recruits are allowed choice of district for assignment. Basic training lasts nine weeks.
Marine Corps	17-28	3 or 4 years	Specialist training, assigned in accordance with Marine Corps needs, is based on determined aptitudes and interests. Qualified personnel can enlist for aviation duty. Basic training is 8-11 weeks.
Army	17-34	2, 3, 4, 5, or 6 years	Enlistment options include guaranteed choice of service school for qualified high school graduates; special duty assignments, training, overseas area assignment, or combinations thereof, for high school and non-high school graduates. Basic training lasts eight weeks.
Navy	17-30	Minority, 4 or 6 years	Minority enlistments for 17-year-olds are held in abeyance until further notice. A 120-day delayed enlistment program is offered. High school graduates and Junior College graduates can select specialty fields for which they are qualified, with guarantee of service school admis-

Service	Ages	Active Duty

sion or formal instruction at a service school level. Junior College and Vocational School graduates may qualify for an advanced pay grade. Basic training is approximately nine weeks.

Service	Ages	Active Duty		
Air Force	17-27	4 years		

Jobs are based on the enlistee's aptitudes and the needs of the Air Force. Basic training lasts six weeks. A Delayed Enlistment Program provides a means by which qualified applicants may enlist in the Air Force Reserve, and within 120 days of the Reserve enlistment date, be called to active duty for regular enlistment for a period of four years. Delayed Enlistment Program enlistees are deferred from the draft while a member of the Air Force Reserve.

II. RESERVE

Service	Ages	Active Duty	Total Time	
Marine Corps	17-26	6 months	6 years	Men must serve 5½ years in the Ready Reserve.
Navy	17-26	2 years	6 years	Can delay active duty for one year after enlisting. Minority enlistments are being held in abeyance.
	17-26	6 months	6 years	Enlistments are limited to those who live within 50 miles of a Naval Air Reserve activity. Minority enlistments are being held in abeyance.
Coast Guard	17-26	5, 6 or 24 months	6 years	Length of active duty depends on the type of specialized training received by the individual.
Air Force	17-34	4 months minimum	6 years	Men must spend remainder of enlistment in the Ready Reserve.

31

Service	Ages	Active Duty	Total Time	
Army	17-26	4 months minimum	6 years	Amount of active duty training depends on specialty for which enlisted. Men must spend remainder of enlistment in the Ready Reserve.
	17-26	2 years	6 years	Men must spend three years in the Ready Reserve and one year in a no training status.
	26-35	4 months minimum	3 years	Amount of active duty training depends on specialty for which enlisted.
Air Force	17-35	4 months minimum	6 years	Men must spend remainder of enlistment in the Ready Reserve.

III. NATIONAL GUARD

Army	17-35	4 months minimum	6 years	Amount of active duty for training depends on specialty for which enlisted.

If the total obligation is not listed for a particular program, it can be assumed that it is six years.

More detailed information about the officer programs and Reserve programs may be found in the HSNS REPORT of September 1968.

IV. AVIATION TRAINING

Air Force	19-26½ years	4 years		Navigator and Pilot Training Programs are open only to commissioned officers.
Army	18-30	*3 years		Warrant Officer Candidate (Army aviator) fixed or rotary wing training program is open to high school graduates, in-service enlisted men and warrant officer personnel.
	18-30	*3 years		Army aviator fixed or rotary wing training program is open to Army officers on active duty.

Service	Ages	Active Duty	
Navy	19-26½	*3½ years	Aviation Officer Candidate Program (pilot) is open to college graduates. (May apply upon completion of junior year of college).
	19-27½	*3½ years	Naval Aviation Officer Candidate Program (non-pilot) is open to college graduates. (May apply upon completion of junior year of College.)
Marine Corps	18-24	*3 years	Platoon Leaders Class (Aviation), PLC (A), is open to college undergraduates.
	20-26	*3½ years	Aviation Officer Candidate Course (AOCC) is open to college graduates.

* after completion of training.

Aviation training programs in the Coast Guard are available to commissioned officers to meet the needs of the service. The Coast Guard Aviation Cadet Program is open to qualified personnel serving in enlisted status in the Coast Guard.

WOMEN IN THE ARMED FORCES

Enlistment requirements for servicewomen are essentially the same in all the armed services. An applicant must have a high school education or its equivalent, be not less than 18 years of age and unmarried, have no dependents, be in good health, and have high moral standards. If under age 21, she must have her parents' or guardian's written consent.

Minimum enlistment periods are: two years in the WAC (Army), three years in the WAVES (Navy) and Women Marines, and four years in the WAF (Air Force). Longer enlistments are optional for all services except the Air Force. In some cases women enlistees can be guaranteed a choice of a specific kind of training.

A servicewoman may marry while on active duty, but may not leave the service for this reason until she has completed a stipulated part of her enlistment. She may not remain on active duty and bear a child.

Professionally qualified women physicians, dentists, nurses, dietitians, physical therapists, occupational therapists, and allied specialists may apply for direct commissions with the Medical Services of the Army, Navy, and Air Force.

Further information about Armed Forces programs for women can be obtained at any of the services' recruiting offices or by writing to:

Commander
U.S. Air Force Recruiting Service
Randolph Air Force Base, Texas   78148

Commanding General
U.S. Army Recruiting Command
Fort Monroe, Va.   23351

Chief of Naval Personnel (Pers B6)
Department of the Navy
Washington, D.C.   20370

Commandant of the Marine Corps
Headquarters, U.S. Marine Corps
Washington, D.C.   20380

Defense Advisory Committee
on Women in the Service OASD (MP & R)
Washington, D.C.   20301

AUXILIARY BENEFITS

Medical care for dependents of active duty and retired personnel at military facilities is authorized when available. Under certain circumstances, it is also authorized at civilian hospitals for dependents of active duty personnel and for retired personnel and their dependents. Routine dental care is authorized for dependents at certain remote installations and overseas.

Enlisted personnel of pay grade E-4 (with at least four years of service) are eligible for military housing. If government housing is available the occupants give up their basic allowance for quarters.

All installations offer military and retired personnel and dependents exchange and commissary privileges where most necessities can be purchased at reduced rates.

BIBLIOGRAPHY

Your Military Obligations and Opportunities by Jack Raymond, new revised edition, N.Y. Collier Books, 1963, 278 pp. paper, 95 cents. Probably the best all-round guide available.
GI Guide: What Every Young American Should Know by Elton Fay, N.Y. Associated Press, 1966, 55 pp. $1.00. Useful information and counsel.
Before You Report for Active Duty, An Official Department of Defense Publication, 6 Dec., 1965 (No. PA-8A); Government Printing Office.

Chapter 5

Routes into Military Service: The Draft

W HATEVER convictions clergymen may have about the Draft
and its manifold implications for American society, it is essential, whether in private counsel or in public debate, that they know
the facts. A huge and growing literature exists. Conscription has become a major contemporary issue. No understanding of young adults
is possible without reference to it. Clergymen are urged to visit draft
boards and to gather pamphlets and books on conscription for their
parishes.

Selective Service has a three-fold responsibility: to register, classify,
and deliver men in numbers requested by the Department of Defense.
The Army examines, accepts, or rejects men furnished by Selective
Service. Here's how the system works.

Registration

Within five days of his eighteenth birthday every male citizen must
register in person at the *nearest* local draft board. His permanent
address determines his local board. Normally, it is not possible to
transfer from one draft board to another. Registration is simple. The
registrar asks a series of identification questions and fills out the form
(SSS 1-A). The registrant reads it or has it read to him and signs his
name. Failure to register can bring heavy fine and imprisonment. The
registrant must keep his board informed of any significant changes in
his personal situation.

Classification

The board sends the registrant a classification questionnaire (SSS-
100) which he must fill out and return within ten days. It will classify
him on the basis of the information he submits. Employers interested
in an occupational deferment should provide supporting information

to be sent in with Form 100. Anyone claiming dependency may submit supplemental data. The registrant may request an opportunity to appear before the board. He may not be represented by a lawyer. *Any person who wishes to register as a conscientious objector should so indicate on his questionnaire.* In all cases, full current information should be supplied in writing. Copies should be kept. If his classification is unsatisfactory, every registrant has a right to a personal appearance and an appeal. His letter of appeal must go to the board not more than thirty days after the board mailed his classification.

SELECTIVE SERVICE CLASSIFICATIONS

CLASS I

Class I-A: Registrant available for military service.

Class I-A-O: Conscientious objector registrant available for noncombatant military service only.

Class I-C: Member of the Armed Forces of the United States, The Coast and Geodetic Survey, or the Public Health Service.

Class I-D: Qualified member of reserve component, or student taking military training, including ROTC and accepted aviation cadet applicant.

Class I-O: Conscientious objector available for civilian work contributing to the maintenance of the national health, safety, or interest.

Class I-S: Student deferred by law until graduation from high school or attainment of age of 20, or until end of his academic year at a college or university.

Class I-W: Conscientious objector performing civilian work contributing to the maintenance of the national health, safety, or interest, or who has completed such work.

Class I-Y: Registrant qualified for military service only in time of war or national emergency.

CLASS II

Class II-A: Occupational deferment (which includes apprentice training).

Class II-C: Agricultural deferment.

Class II-S: Student deferment.

CLASS III

Class III-A: Extreme hardship deferment, or registrant with a child or children.

CLASS IV

Class IV-A: Registrant with sufficient prior active service or who is a sole surviving son.
Class IV-B: Official deferred by law.
Class IV-C: Alien not currently liable for military service.
Class IV-D: Minister of religion or divinity student.
Class IV-F: Registrant not qualified for any military service.

CLASS V

Class V-A: Registrant over the age of liability for military service.

SPECIAL NOTICE: A registrant who was deferred on or before his 26th birthday has his liability extended to his 35th birthday.

Induction

A young man classified I-A is notified when and where to report for pre-induction tests. These include an Armed Forces Qualification Test (AFQT). Given by the Army (*not* Selective Service), they are based on criteria established by the Secretary of Defense. Upon passing the tests, the registrant receives a Certificate of Acceptability (DD-62). If he does not pass them, he may be declared either qualified for military service in a national emergency (I-Y) or not qualified at any time (IV-F). Homosexuality is a certain ground for disqualification. Note that by law

a) A man cannot be inducted before he is 18½, unless he volunteers.
b) Induction may not occur earlier than 21 days after the mailing of the Certificate of Acceptability.
c) Ten days' notice of an induction date is required.
d) Before a man is sworn in he receives another physical examination at the induction station.

The law also stipulates the order in which men are inducted. Generally, this is (1) Delinquents, (2) Volunteers, (3) Nonvolunteers, age 19-25, single or married after August 26, 1965, (4) Nonvolunteers, age 19-25, married on or before August 26, 1965, (5) Nonvolunteers, age 26 and older, and (6) Nonvolunteers age 18½ to 19.

Men are inducted for twenty-four months of active duty, after which come six years in the Ready Reserve, subject to recall by Presidential Order. Men in Reserve units may count on at least six months of active duty.

DEFERMENTS

A deferment is a delay in call to service, not a permanent exemption, and is granted by the local board when it believes this will best serve the nation's health, safety, or interest. The law prohibits blanket deferments. Certain deferments may be renewed. Others may not, and none is for more than a year at a time. New information or changed circumstances, such as withdrawal from school, may justify reconsideration of a deferment. Types of deferments in effect in mid-1968 are as follows:

I. Student. These are of two kinds, statutory and authorized by regulation (alterable) within fixed statutory limits. The first permits a student to complete high school or an academic year in college. (I-S). The ROTC student (I-D) is also deferred by law.

The second type (II-S) is for the general college student. The registrant may request that he be deferred to attend college. He may do so by letter or by SSS Form 104. To qualify, he must (a) be engaged in a full-time course of study leading to an academic degree; (b) be making progress at a rate which will enable him to complete his studies in the normal period of time. Boards usually take special circumstances into consideration. The II-S deferment may be renewed at the discretion of the board until he "receives his baccalaureate degree, ceases to perform satisfactorily, or attains the age of twenty-four."

In February, 1968 Selective Service announced that there would be no further deferments for graduate students in any field, other than in medicine, dentistry, or divinity, except in the cases of students having completed two or more years of such study by June, 1968.

II. Conscientious Objection. This subject is taken up in Chapter 6.

III. Men Already in the Services. These are classified I-C.

IV. Occupational Deferments. At the end of 1967, 339,474 persons were deferred because their work was deemed vital to the national interest. Recent policy announcements suggest that II-A deferments may be restricted in 1968. Local boards utilize lists of "currently critical" occupations supplied by the Departments of Commerce and Labor. Badly needed agricultural workers are deferred (II-C).

V. Hardship. In cases where induction would impose extreme hardship upon dependents a board may grant the III-A Classification. It may be available to registrants with a child or children. Nearly, 4,000,000 men were classified III-A in December, 1967.

VI. Those Not Currently Qualified. Those who do not pass the physical, mental, or moral tests at their pre-induction examination are classified I-Y. In time of war or national emergency many men now rejected would be accepted. This classification is thus a refinement of the IV-F category. It provides a "readily identifiable source of available manpower which has been processed and whose probable utilization potential has been predetermined."

VII. Special Deferments. These are reserved for: (1) the sole surviving son of a family which has lost a son or daughter while serving in the Armed Forces; (2) public officials; (3) certain aliens; (4) ministers of religion and divinity students; and (5) those found unfit for any military service at any time; (6) registrants over the age of liability for military service.

LOCATING SELECTIVE SERVICE PERSONNEL

In the capital city of each State, in New York City, and in the Panama Canal Zone, Guam, Puerto Rico, and the Virgin Islands there is a Director of Selective Service. His headquarters is listed in the appropriate telephone directory under "U.S. Government, Selective Service System." Local Board listings are included.

The National Director of Selective Service is Lt. General Lewis B. Hershey, 1724 F. St. N.W., Washington, D.C. 20435.

Postscript

The writer again urges clergymen to familiarize themselves with the "problem" of the draft as it stands before the public in 1968. To say that it troubles young Americans more than any other single issue understates the case. Aside from the question of the very existence of conscription, the present statute and its administration leave much to be desired. Clergymen ought to study carefully the report of the National Advisory Commission on Selective Service, commonly called the "Marshall Commission" after its chairman, Mr. Burke Marshall. This asserts that "The United States has outgrown its Selective Service System," [1] and effectively documents its statement.

The Marshall Commission believes that there is no likelihood that the draft will disappear. It urges retention of Selective Service, but in a modernized form. Even without the Vietnam War, experts do not expect our active forces to dip much below 2.5 million. They agree also that an army of this size cannot be maintained solely by voluntary

---

[1] p. 17. Available at U.S. Government Printing Office, Wash. D.C.

enlistments. Many believe that it is far healthier and in accord with American traditions to maintain forces comprised of short-term citizen soldiers rather than of well-paid professionals. To obtain military manpower in crisis situations the government needs a conscription apparatus, even though on a stand-by basis.

In a society half of whose members are under twenty-five, however, the number of men available far exceeds the number needed. Since our tradition lays the burden of service equally upon all citizens, the dilemma such a situation creates is well expressed by the title of the Marshall report: "In Pursuit of Equity: Who Serves When Not All Serve?" It recommends a system of random selection which would in fact put each registrant in equal risk of being called. This is true now only in theory. Opponents argue that such a system would (a) be administratively too difficult, and (b) constitute an abandonment of the rational selection deemed important to determination of the national health, safety, and interest. The problem was not resolved by passage of the Military Selective Service Act of June 30, 1967. Many believe that this measure worsened an already poor situation. The Congress has rejected all proposals to modify its 1967 statute.

Those who counsel young men ought to urge them to plan ahead as to how they will meet their obligation to military service. Many, many possibilities exist. Eighteen-year-olds can arrive at Draft Registration Day with a well-considered course of action. The appearance of draft counseling centers throughout the country is a belated response to a long-existing need. The importance of familiarity with Selective Service laws and procedures by civilian clergymen cannot be overemphasized.

TOTAL ACTIVE DUTY MILITARY PERSONNEL IN THE UNITED STATES, 1916-1960[1]

Period	Number	Ratio of Change[a]
Pre-World War I		
June 30, 1916	179,376	226
World War I peak		
November 11, 1918	4,315,239	24
Post-World War I low		
June 30, 1933	243,845	.06

40

Period	Number	Ratio of Change[a]
Pre-World War II		
June 30, 1939	334,473	1.4
World War II peak		
May 31, 1945	12,124,418	36
Post-World War II low		
May 31, 1948	1,398,726	.12
Korean Conflict Peak		
April 30, 1952	3,685,054	2.6
Post-Korean Conflict		
June 30, 1960	2,476,435	.67

SOURCE: Statistics issued by the Statistical Services Center, Office of Secretary of Defense, August 19, 1960.

[a] Strength in the given period as ratio of strength in preceding period.

[1] Cited in *The New Military* edited by Morris Janowitz, N.Y. The Russell Sage Foundation, 1964, p. 41 (paper, $2.65).

BIBLIOGRAPHY

Peacetime Conscription by Julia E. Johnson, a debate handbook, The Reference Shelf, Vol. 18 No. 4, N.Y. H. W. Wilson Co., 1945. Includes a long bibliography, many articles, pro and con.

Universal Conscription for Essential Service by Herbert L. Marz, The Reference Shelf, Vol. 23, No. 3, N.Y. H. W. Wilson Co., 1951. Contains speech by Senator Robert Taft opposing compulsory military training in peacetime.

The French Theory of the Nation in Arms, 1866-1939 by Richard D. Challener, N.Y. Columbia University Press, 1955. About conscription in France and its political and economic consequences. Shows how France was unable to face Hitler's 1935 occupation of the Rhineland without total mobilization.

The Military Establishment by John M. Swomley, Boston, Beacon Hill Press, 1964. Case study of campaign for and against Universal Military Training with chapter on Selective Conscription and Compulsory Reserve. Includes chapters on military influence in American life.

Outline of Historical Background of Selective Service and Chronology by Lt. General Lewis B. Hershey, Pamphlet, revised, 1965, 66 pp. U.S. Government Printing Office: 1966 0-209-841. Events to June 30, '65.

Selective Service, monthly bulletin of Selective Service System, Office of Public Information, Washington, D.C. 20435.

Report of the National Conference on the Draft, 11-12 Nov., 1966. Available from the American Veterans Committee, 1830 Jefferson Place, N.W., Washington, D.C.   20036.

The Draft: Handbook of Facts and Alternatives by Prof. Sol Tax, University of Chicago Press, Findings of a Conference on the Draft held in Chicago, Dec. 4-7, 1966.

A Considered Comment on Selective Service by Colin W. Bell, testimony of the Executive Secretary of the American Friends Service Committee before the Marshall Commission, Nov. 2, 1966. AFSC, 160 North 15th St., Philadelphia, Pa.   19102.

The Universal Military Obligation by John Graham, N.Y. Fund for the Republic, 1958. Presents inequities of the present draft and suggests desirability of ending it.

Baldwin, Hanson W., "The Draft Is Here to Stay, But It Should Be Changed," Article, *N.Y. Times Magazine,* Nov. 20, 1966, pp. 48-49.

Davidson, B., "Hell, No, We Won't Go" Article, *Saturday Evening Post,* 241:21-26, January 27, 1968.

"Four Ways to Go: The Route Taken by Four Students in the Draft." *Esquire,* September, 1966, pp. 109 ff.

Mead, Margaret, "The Case for Drafting All Boys and Girls" Article, *Redbook,* September, 1966, pp. 40 ff.

The literature on the Draft is now enourmous

Chapter 6

Conscientious Objection

A CENTRAL axiom of religion is that conscience must ultimately guide responsible human action. Society and governments have strong reason to encourage citizens to live according to the highest dictates of conscience. Yet, with respect to war in particular, the promptings of conscience can lead men of integrity to opposite conclusions. It can divide good men very deeply. Nevertheless, the pastoral obligation of the church is clear. Her ministry to those entering or in Armed Forces must include both conscientious participant *and* conscientious objector.

In the space allotted this chapter can barely skim its subject, let alone explore the mysterious well-springs of conscience. What follows is based largely on *The Handbook for Conscientious Objectors*.[1] The serious CO and anyone who attempts to counsel him will *require* this publication. The counseling task itself is analyzed in Chapter 2.

Get Help!

The young man who seeks CO status will usually need mature, competent assistance. He will require factual information on the draft law; he will need to talk over his beliefs and to know his rights and responsibilities. He may need experienced legal counsel. He may require help in finding civilian service suitable to his background and abilities. Finally, he will need a friend to help him know his own mind and the course of action which is right for him. Numerous agencies are prepared to offer assistance. Three of the best are

The American Friends Service Committee
160 N. 15th Street, Philadelphia, Pa.   19102

[1] Published by the Central Committee for Conscientious Objectors, 9th ed. Jan. 1968, 110 pp. $1. (Hereafter called the *CCCO Handbook*)

The Central Committee for Conscientious Objectors
2016 Walnut Street, Philadelphia, Pa.   19103, or
4371 Market Street, San Francisco, Calif.   94105
Its subsidiary, the Midwest Committee for Draft Counseling,
179 N. Michigan Ave., Chicago, Ill.   60601

The National Service Board for Religious Objectors
550 Washington Building
15th Street and New York Ave., N.W.
Washington, D.C.   20005

The American Friends Service Committee also has ten regional offices
in various parts of the country. The services of the above groups are
free and nonsectarian. Other regional, denominational, and local
groups are at work. The National Lawyer's Guild, 5 Beekman St.,
New York, N.Y.   10038, offers legal assistance. So does the American
Civil Liberties Union, 156 5th Ave., New York, N.Y.   10016. The
CCCO can supply any CO with the name and address of the resource
nearest him. He should not wait until the last minute to obtain assistance. In his first letter he should provide full information about himself, viz. date of birth, a complete chronological record of all dealings
with Selective Service, and a copy of answers given to the questions
on the Special Form for Conscientious Objectors (SSS 150). The
following general rules should be observed:

1. Keep copies of everything sent to the local board; keep everything
   received from it.
2. Make all requests, appeals, etc. in writing. Mail by certified letter.
   Keep receipts.
3. Accept no oral promises from draft board personnel. Follow printed
   instructions explicitly.
4. Present as full a case as possible to the draft board. Omit no relevant
   points in hearings or correspondence.
5. Observe deadlines, especially on appeals. Report changes of address
   promptly. Appeal whenever in doubt.
6. If the board suggests an appointment with its Appeals Agent or
   Advisor to Registrants, obtain one. Write a detailed, factual report
   of any such interview. Keep a copy.
7. If away from home, have mail forwarded promptly or opened for you.
   If abroad, give your board an address.
8. Know what you believe; if in doubt, get help.

The CO Proviso in the Military Selective Service Act of 1967
Nothing contained in this title shall be construed to require any person

44

to be subject to combatant training and service in the armed forces of the United States who, by reason of religious training and belief, is conscientiously opposed to participation in war in any form. As used in this subsection, the term 'religious training and belief' does not include essentially political, sociological, or philosophical views or a merely personal moral code. Any person claiming exemption from combatant training and service because of such conscientious objections whose claim is sustained by the local board shall, if he is inducted into the armed forces under this title, be assigned to noncombatant service as defined by the President, or shall, if he is found to be conscientiously opposed to participation in such noncombatant service, in lieu of such induction, be ordered by his local board, subject to such regulations as the President may prescribe, to perform for a period equal to the period prescribed in section 4(b) such civilian work contributing to the maintenance of the national health, safety, or interest as the local board pursuant to Presidential regulations may deem appropriate . . . [Act, sec. 6(j)]

Procedure for CO Classification

The conscientious objector's first opportunity to indicate his belief officially comes when he fills out the Classification Questionnaire (SSS Form No. 100), on page 4:

I claim to be a conscientious objector by reason of my religious training and belief and therefore request the local board to furnish me a Special Form for Conscientious Objector (SSS Form 150).

Form 150 should be completed and returned within ten days of the date it was mailed. It is on the basis of the information supplied on this form, with any attached supplemental statements, that the board will grant or refuse the application. Great care should be taken in filling out Form 150. Detailed advice is offered on pp. 13-16 of the *CCCO Handbook*. The registrant should think his position through carefully and be prepared for some rough questioning; an interview may be required. An experienced advisor can help.

To Appeal an Unfavorable Decision

If the applicant is refused his I-O or I-A-O Classification he must act at once. He has the right to appear in person before the "member or members of the local board designated for the purpose if he files a written request therefor within 30 days after the local board has mailed a Notice of Classification to him. Such 30-day period may not be extended" [Sect. 1624.1 (a), SSS Regulations].

He should request a hearing and bring with him a witness who is prepared to speak on his behalf. The witness should not be a relative, and facts should be his concern. He should make it clear that his opinions have not unduly influenced the applicant.

Following this hearing the board considers the case anew and makes its decision. If this also is unfavorable, the registrant now has the right to file a written appeal, and must do so within 30 days. It should be sent to the local board which in turn will forward it to the State Appeal Board. Prior to July 1, 1967 appeals were referred to the Department of Justice for an advisory opinion. THIS IS NO LONGER TRUE. The State Board decides and notifies the local board. If the vote of the Appeal Board was unanimous the registrant has no further appeal rights. Should there have been division within the Board, the registrant may appeal "to the President"—actually to a three-member civilian National Selective Service Appeal Board. Registrants cannot be inducted while appeals are pending.

COs Facing Induction

Any registrant who has exhausted his appeal rights and who has been physically examined and found acceptable for service, may be ordered for induction. His only recourse, if he will not obey the induction order, is to defend himself in the courts by attacking the Selective Service order as illegal. The CO in this predicament should obtain legal aid immediately. He will do well to notify one of the resource agencies listed on pp. 43, 44 of this book (cf. pp. 41-73 of *The CCCO Handbook*).

Noncombatant Duty: The CO Within the Armed Forces

Many COs accept noncombatant duty and perform creditably. Many have been decorated. I-A-Os inducted into the Army go to the Medical Training Center at Ft. Sam Houston, San Antonio, Texas. Their basic training lasts for sixteen weeks, eight for standard basic training (without weapons), and eight for individual training, chiefly in medical subjects. The CO is thus prepared for front-line duty—to which he is just as likely to be assigned as the non-CO. It must be remembered that though the immediate duties of the unarmed medical corpsman are essentially humanitarian, their overriding aim is to contribute to the success of the command. The medic is a soldier, and his ultimate object is to help win battles. Army medical manuals are explicit about this.

Obtaining CO Status While on Active Duty; CO Discharge

Some men become COs after entrance into the Armed Forces. Their situation is discouraging. Nevertheless, applicants should

1. Make written application under the appropriate regulation to the commanding officer. The request should include a clear statement of the basis for the position taken as well as how it developed.
2. If a member of a church, obtain a letter from the pastor attesting membership and stating either that the beliefs of the church or the CO's own convictions do not permit him to perform combat duty. Also, three letters from friends.
3. If not a member of a church, or if the position held has a non-religious basis, secure three or more letters from friends and associates vouching for the sincerity of the claim.

Petitioners are interviewed by the chaplain and the commander (and possibly by others). During the processing period they *must* be assigned to noncombatant duty. It is likely that the CO whose request for noncombatant duty has been denied and who refuses to obey subsequent orders will be arrested, court-martialed, and imprisoned. The resource agencies already mentioned will help as they can.

Though there is military procedure for seeking discharge on ground of conscience, the prospects are dismal. Since the Spring of 1966 virtually all applications have been denied.

Civilian Employment

Registrants gaining I-O status are assigned jobs with approved employers. Usually they work in the field of public health or welfare, including related educational and scientific activity. Private employment for profit-making organizations is forbidden (cf. *CCCO Handbook*, pp. 30-33).

"Selective" Conscientious Objection

The Vietnam War has led a growing number of Americans to believe that the Government should expand its recognition of conscientious objection to include objection in conscience to a particular war, though not to all war. The World Council of Churches endorsed this alleged right of "selective" objection at its meeting in Uppsala, Sweden in July, 1968. Several denominations have officially sanctioned it; some have opposed. The Marshall Commission, in its far-reaching study of Selective Service released in February, 1967, declined to recommend such an extension of the present statute (cf. pp. 49-50 of its report, *In Pursuit of Equity: Who Serves When Not All Serve?*) This subject will receive much attention as an aspect of draft law reform. There is space here only to urge churchmen to "bone up" on it. Some reading suggestions are given at the close of the chapter.

National Service

In recent years the Peace Corps, Vista, the National Teachers Corps, and other volunteer service programs have won an honored place in American life. They reflect the developing interest in what has come to be known as "national service," the proposition that "the young men and women of America owe to their country, or to their fellow man, or to themselves some period of service in the public interest." The Marshall Commission considered this contention and concluded that "no fair way exists, at least at present, to equate non-military service with military service," and that "selective service, which rests upon military needs, should not be confused with the concept of civilian voluntary service, which rests upon educational and social needs" (cf. pp. 61-3 of its report).

In one form or another, "national service" programs exist in thirty-three countries. The National Service Secretariat, Suite 500, 1629 K Street, N.W., Washington, D.C. 20006, conducts research, provides information, and offers consultative services.

"Just" War Doctrine

For an extensive treatment of this venerable subject, see the article under "War" in the *New Catholic Encyclopedia*, N.Y., McGraw-Hill, 1967, Vol. 14, pp. 795-807, especially under the heading "Morality of War," pp. 802-807.

BIBLIOGRAPHY

An extensive listing of books on Conscientious Objection will be found on pp. 98-106 of *The CCCO Handbook.*
The Dawn of Conscience by James H. Breasted, N.Y.C. Scribner's & Sons, 1934, 431 pp. ill.
The Early Christian Attitude to War by C. John Cadoux, London, Allen & Unwin, 1940, 265 pp. Examines the earliest Christian writings and practices; shows how the Church came to terms with the State.
God, Man and Atomic War by Samuel Dresner, N.Y. Living Books, 1966, 277 pp. On the relevance of Judaism to the war-peace debate. $5.75.

Concerning Dissent and Civil Disobedience by Abe Fortas. Signet Books, 1968. 64 pp. 50 cents.

The Power of Non-Violence by Richard Gregg, 2nd revised ed.; foreword by Martin Luther King, Jr.; Nyack, N.Y. Fellowship Publications, 1959, 192 pp. A standard work on the application of non-violence to conflict situations.

"The Just War and the Selective Objector," Art. by Alan Geyer in *Christian Century*, 2/16/66, pp. 199-201.

The New Testament Basis of Pacifism by G.H.C. Macregor, revised ed. & *The Relevance of an Impossible Ideal*, Nyack, N.Y. Fellowship Publications, 1960, the first, a standard book on pacifist interpretation of the New Testament; the latter a strong reply to Niebuhr (below).

Non Violence in an Aggressive World by A. J. Muste, Nyack, N.Y. Fellowship Publications, 1944, 211 pp. & *Not By Might*, N.Y. Harper Bros., 1947, 227 pp. By America's most famous pacifist.

Christianity and Power Politics by Reinhold Niebuhr, N.Y. Charles Scribner's Sons, 1940, 226 pp. Holds that Christian perfectionism which places a premium upon non-participation in conflict is a sentimentalized version of the Christian faith.

Statements of Religious Bodies on the Conscientious Objector, Washington, D.C. National Service Board for Religious Objectors, 1966, 59 pp.

Civil Disobedience by David Henry Thoreau, widely available; the classic exposition of the individual's duty to refuse cooperation with evil.

Conscientious Objection by U.S. Selective Service System, Washington, D.C., Government Printing Office, 1950, 2 Vols. 625 pp. Our government's record of its dealings with objectors to World War II.

War Conscience and Dissent by Gordon C. Zahn, Hawthorn Press, 1967. A Catholic sociologist's case for pacifism within the context of the teachings of his church.

Testimony on Selective Conscientious Objection, leaflet reprint of statement of the Rev. Dr. Roger L. Shinn to Senate Armed Services Committee; United Church of Christ, 289 Park Ave., South, N.Y.C. 10010.

A Profile of National Service by Donald J. Eberly, Booklet, Overseas Educational Service, 522 Fifth Ave., N.Y.C. 10036, 60 pp. Includes an historically arranged bibliography on the emergence of national service.

War and Conscience in America by Edward LeRoy Long, Jr. Westminster Press. 1968. 130 pp. $1.65 (paper). An excellent new study of an ancient issue.

Chapter 7

Speaking Up for the Serviceman:
A Reply to Critics of Military Service

THE hostility of many clergymen, academicians, and others to the Vietnam policy of the United States Government is an understandable expression of opinion within a society which has thrived upon respect for honest, responsible dissent. It remains, of course, for history to determine whether the policy or its critics are correct. This determination is not the writer's present concern. What does trouble him is the widespread tendency to misdirect this antagonism—i.e. from the framers of American policy to those who are its servants, specifically, members of the Armed Forces. The distinction between President and private may be a moot one for many angry young men; the soldier's lot, like that of his kinsman, the policeman, has never been a happy one. Because of Vietnam he has been reviled—spat upon, taunted, and jeered to an unconscionable degree by vehement young Americans, in some cases with the open approbation of their elders, clerical and lay. Though serving with greater distinction and higher morale than ever before in U.S. history, members of the Armed Forces have been pictured as dupes of a war-mad Government, encouraged to desert, and made to wonder if indeed they might be aliens to their own countrymen. However easy it may be to seize upon the nearest instrument of a detested policy, all of this is wrong. In another era it produced this bitter poem:

TOMMY[1]
By Rudyard Kipling

I went into a public 'ouse to get a pint o' beer,
The publican 'e up an' sez, 'We serve no red-coats here.'
The girls be'ind the bar they laughed an' giggled fit to die,
I outs into the street again an' to myself sez I:

O it's Tommy this, an' Tommy that,
    an' 'Tommy, go away';
But it's 'Thank you, Mister Atkins,'
    when the band begins to play,
The band begins to play, my boys,
    the band begins to play,
O it's 'Thank you, Mister Atkins,'
    when the band begins to play.

I went into a theatre as sober as could be,
They gave a drunk civilian room, but 'adn't none for me;
They sent me to the gallery or round the music-'alls,
But when it comes to fightin', Lord! they'll shove me in the stalls!

Yes, makin' mock o' uniforms that guard you while you sleep
Is cheaper than them uniforms, an' they're starvation cheap;
An' hustlin' drunken soldiers when they're goin' large a bit
Is five times better business than paradin' in full kit.

    Then it's Tommy this, an' Tommy
        that, an' 'Tommy, 'ow's yer soul?'
    But it's 'Thin red line of 'eroes'
        when the drums begin to roll,
    The drums begin to roll, my boys,
        the drums begin to roll,
    O it's 'Thin red line of 'eroes' when
        the drums begin to roll.

We aren't no thin red 'eroes, nor we aren't no blackguards too,
But single men in barricks, most remarkable like you;
An' if sometimes our conduck isn't all your fancy paints:
Why, single men in barricks don't grow into plaster saints;

    For it's Tommy this, an' Tommy that,
        an' 'Chuck him out, the brute!'
    But it's 'Saviour of 'is country,' when
        the guns begin to shoot;
    Yes it's Tommy this, an' Tommy
        that, an' anything you please;
    But Tommy ain't a bloomin' fool—
        you bet that Tommy sees!

[1] From *Departmental Ditties and Barrack-Room Ballads,* Doubleday & Co., Inc.; abridged by permission.

Such scorning of the serviceman creates a bitter legacy. Few GIs or officers forget how civilians treated them as "second class citizens" and "first class outsiders." "Sailors and dogs, keep off the grass!" may have been an apocryphal sign in an old Navy town, but it bespeaks actual experience.

His Mission Is Peace

Such rude behavior is tantamount to blaming the soldier for the existence of war. Though it may be a paradox, peace-keeping is in fact of greater work-a-day concern to him than it is to most civilians. His role as a maintainer of peace is instilled in his consciousness throughout his tour of duty. Some may scoff at such a claim, but others, in and outside of the U.S.A., know that any disappearance of America's armed forces would everywhere be a disaster to the cause of peace. Let governments bear the blame for war; give some to munitions makers and profit-hungry industrial combines, to their directors and stockholders; let even the military professionals, with their own vested interests, have their just part of it;[2] let us share in it, since there is warfare in our hearts, but let the GI, insofar as his military employment is concerned, be freed from the epithet of "War-Monger!" His is an honorable profession, and it should be respected.

Respected in Scripture

Unquestionably, the Bible is devoted to peace. For Christians its central figure is Jesus, the Prince of Peace. Yet, precisely because the Scriptures are an honest reflection of human life, war is one of the most prominent biblical themes, especially in the Old Testament. Maxims, illustrations, and exhortations derived from military life are commonplace. Martial analogies abound in the writings of St. Paul. Scholars have traced the evolution of warfare in the Bible as well as the development of biblical attitudes toward it.[3] Clearly, the Scriptures do not glorify war. But neither do they excoriate the soldier. On the contrary, they accept and respect him.

Soldiers figure prominently in the Gospels. They were among those who responded to the preaching of John the Baptist (Luke 3:14).

[2] For an illuminating sociological study of the military calling, see *The Professional Soldier: A Social and Political Portrait*, by Morris Janowitz; N.Y. Free Press, 1960, 464 pp. Esp. Chapter 18.

[3] cf. *The Interpreter's Dictionary of the Bible*, Vol. 4 pp. 796-805; N.Y. Abingdon, 1962.

"What can we do?" they asked. Jesus lived in a land ruled by an army of occupation. Encounters with soldiers were a part of daily life. On one occasion he ministered to a centurion and came to hold him in the highest regard. With astonishment he heard the officer say, "I am used to working under orders, and I have soldiers under me. I say to one, 'Go,' and he goes, and to another, 'Come,' and he comes. Say the word only, and my servant shall be healed" (Luke 7:1-10). Jesus turned in amazement to the crowd and said, "I have never found faith like this anywhere, even in Israel!" He did not reproach the centurion for his occupation or regard him as being beyond the pale. Rather, he accepted him as a person and helped him at his point of need. In the process he won an undying gratitude and, doubtless, a life-long disciple.

Soldiers participated in the tragic drama of Jesus' trial before Pilate and carried out the governor's order that he be executed. According to St. Luke, at least one of them was both perceptive and reverent. "That indeed was a good man!" (23:47).

Another centurion, Cornelius, became the means by which Peter was brought to realize that the gospel is for all mankind. As a direct result of his disconcerting experience with Cornelius at Caesarea, Peter later threw the decisive weight of his support behind Paul's startling proposal to launch an apostolate to non-Jews. The decision of that first Christian synod at Jerusalem was momentous. It started Paul and Barnabas on their crucial mission to the Gentiles. Thus, it may fairly be claimed that the development of Christianity in the West had its roots in an Apostle's ministering to a Roman officer on occupation duty in Palestine (Acts 10, 15).

St. Paul's Use of Military Imagery

To prepare its members for the perilous task of witnessing to the Lord in an intensely hostile world, the early Christian community drew upon its daily experience with soldiers. Since by the Master's specific instruction and example it could not campaign for a worldly political kingdom, its concept of warfare was spiritualized. Nonetheless, warfare it was. St. Paul sounded an immortal call to arms:

Be strong . . . in the Lord . . . Put on God's complete armor so that you can successfully resist all the devil's methods of attack. For . . . our fight is not against any physical enemy: it is against organizations and powers that are spiritual. We are up against the unseen power that controls this dark

53

world, and spiritual agents from the very headquarters of evil. Therefore you must wear the whole armor of God that you may be able to resist evil in its day of power, and that even when you have fought to a standstill you may still stand your ground. Take your stand then with truth as your belt, righteousness your breastplate, the gospel of peace firmly on your feet, salvation as your helmet and in your hand the sword of the Spirit, the Word of God. Above all be sure you take faith as your shield, for it can quench every burning missile the enemy hurls at you. (Eph. 6:10 ff.—Phillips)

This is but the most striking of St. Paul's many military allusions. A few others may be listed here:

Unless the bugle note is clear who will be called to arms? (1 Corinthians 14:8)

. . . the battle we are fighting is on the spiritual level. The very weapons we use are not those of human warfare but powerful in God's warfare for the destruction of the enemy's strongholds. Our battle is to bring down every deceptive fantasy and every imposing defense that men erect against the true knowledge of God. . . (2 Corinthians 10:1 ff.)

Put up with your share of hardship as a loyal soldier in Christ's army. Remember: That no soldier on active service gets himself entangled in business, or he will not please his commanding officer. . ." (2 Timothy 2:1)

Thus, not only does the New Testament faithfully record the soldier as part of the daily scene, but it borrows from his milieu to delineate exemplary Christian conduct. It appeals to the martial instinct even as it spiritualizes it.

Soldier-Missionaries
History records that soldiers have planted the seed of the Gospel during campaigns all over the world. Anglican Christians honor Alban, a Roman soldier, as Britain's first martyr. Many a mission church, hospital, and school owes its founding to Christian soldiers. Cardinal Spellman has pointed out that his church has among its canonized saints "more soldiers than from any other profession." [4] "Saintly" is not a term normally applicable to soldiers in any era. One must not presume upon the Cardinal's reference, but it is certainly interesting.

[4] Quoted from *National Catholic Community Service Prayerbook for Servicemen and Servicewomen,* 1959, p. 72.

It Is Not Otherwise Today

There are many deeply religious men in the Armed Forces; their military calling has, if anything, strengthened their faith. They serve both country and church with deepened insight and devotion. They continue their works of mercy and rehabilitation. One must always judge by the best and not the worst examples. The great majority of our military men are highly motivated. They take their heavy responsibilities most seriously. They are not callous butchers, but dedicated citizens of a great Republic.

In point of fact, the armed services have made and are continuing to make a major contribution to the development of a great many young men on a great many different fronts—in terms of education, occupation, health, social skills, and general personal development. Indicative of the American public's attitude toward military service is the fact that this wide impact of the armed services on youth has largely gone unnoticed . . .[5]

Their country will need them for years to come as, in the meantime, international society moves toward the establishment of an effective world government. In the world of the future, the keeping of peace will continue to involve soldiers—a paradox, yes, but true withal. Already, they have served the United Nations with distinction.

The Edifice of Peace

The qualities of persevering good will, openness to reason, and all the winsome traits embodied in the "love of Christ" as Christians understand it and as St. Paul expounded it in 1 Corinthians 13 form a leaven without which peace cannot come to this distraught planet. Yet, by themselves alone they cannot accomplish the result for which millions pray. They open the gate to the Promised Land; they do not build the kingdom. Vastly more than "goodwill among men" is needed to bring "peace on earth." The coming of stability, security, justice, freedom, health, and opportunity for all to grow and develop—which is what "peace on earth" really means—will require the skills and labors of hosts of "technocrats"—diplomats, economists, planners, lawyers, administrators, scientists, engineers, doctors, tradesmen, artisans, clerks, laborers, and innumerable other specialists, soldiers not excluded. We should not lose sight of this limitation to what unaided

[5] Ginzberg, *The Optimistic Tradition and American Youth*, pp. 81-2; *op. cit.*

brotherly love can accomplish. The "technical competence of religion is narrow. The work of construction, whether of buildings or of communities, requires skill and involves logistical considerations as well as good will—and probably in almost equal proportion. We must acknowledge more readily the common dependence on the many workmen who must construct the edifice of world peace and appreciate more fully the burden which the possession of power imposes upon its holder.[6]

Power remains one of the harsh realities of the modern world. The very word conjures up a collateral reality—balances of power—which, in an imperfect world, implies the need for a military apparatus—for soldiers. Without them the world as it now is could not proceed to the world that shall be hereafter.

The intent of the foregoing pages is not to claim that soldiers are better than other men, but merely that they are no worse, and that they make an important and ultimately constructive contribution to the common life. At this moment in American history it is time that Christians spoke a word of encouragement and of appreciation to those who do indeed "guard us while we sleep."

[6] cf. Alan R. Booth, *Not Only Peace*, N.Y. Seabury Press, 1967, 142 pp. for a "Christian exploration of the Twentieth Century meaning of power." (esp. Chapter 2, "The Dangers of Moralizing")

Chapter 8

Things the Congregation Can Do

WHETHER involvement begets concern or concern involvement may be debated; what is certain is that concerned persons are at the core of every effective ministry. A ready-made "Armed Forces involvement" exists in every community and congregation in the persons of veterans of military service and of the families and friends of servicemen. These all share a "live" interest in the Armed Forces. Very often, they have firsthand experience. They will respond gratefully to the clergyman's summons to Armed Forces work. Individually and collectively they can do an amazing job. A group is better because it can address itself to the various facets of the work with greater thoroughness. The total burden is shared. This is true particularly when the congregation is large and has many servicemen among its members.

Except for draft counseling, little or no training is needed. Hospitality continues to be a major element, and churches need no instruction here. Many shut-ins and invalids are excellent letter writers. What is essential is that those involved be lively, friendly, imaginative, and young in outlook. Thoughtfulness and the ability to perceive another's situation sympathetically are important. So is a good store of common sense. Conversational ability helps. Older people who remember their own days of military service or whose sons and daughters are in uniform are delighted to be asked to "join up." The normal organizing skills of Americans are ample for this work.

A few things should be borne in mind. One is the factor of transiency. Servicemen are here today and in Saigon or Asmara tomorrow. They are perhaps the best-known exemplars of an American phenomenon—mobility. The Bureau of the Census estimates that one family in five, between eleven and twelve million families, 40,000,000 people, move each year. Churches must know how to minister to nomads.

57

Another factor is the age level of the 3.4 million now in uniform. It averages twenty. The churches must address themselves to young men and women.[1] This will take thought—plus patience and perseverance. Not all servicemen, however, are young and single. Thousands are young and recently married. They struggle to adjust simultaneously to a new relationship and to the demands of military service. They do it far away from familiar scenes and persons. The young bride works. A child may be on the way. Still other thousands are older, with children in their teens or in college. They may live on the post or off it in a near-by community. They may have moved a dozen times in as many years. Many are approaching retirement. In Armed Forces work the accent is on youth, but there is a wide variety. Programs must meet differing needs.

A final caution must be the reminder that in the Armed Forces ministry proselyting is out of order. The demonstration of genuine interest and concern speaks for itself, and the congregation need not press its own interests any further. Military personnel experience enough exploitation on weekdays. They will not take kindly to more of the same on Sunday.

The congregation's Armed Forces Committee can establish programs on the subject of conscription. It can ensure that literature on the draft as well as mature counselors are available to young people, whether of the congregation or of the community. This can grow into a very large undertaking. Chapter Two deals with it more fully.

Take Notice of Enlistment or Induction

Every congregation will wish to note publicly the entrance of its young people into military service. Very often it never learns that "Johnny" has gone. Someone—Johnny, his family, a friend, or the parish committee—needs to tell the clergyman enough ahead of time to enable him to recognize Johnny during a service and present him with a suitable gift—a Bible, prayer book, or medal. Many denominations have these prepared expressly for servicemen. From this time onward Johnny's name will be on the parish Honor Roll.

While They're on Active Duty

What can the home-town congregation do for the young man or woman who has gone off to military duty? One answer is "Very little." It has already had its opportunity. Like the teacher, it must now wait

[1] See Ch. 1.

58

and see what lessons it has communicated to its pupil. Its ability to influence a young life is now to be tested. It can, however, even from a distance, continue to show that it cares. Here are some suggestions for the parish Armed Forces Chairman and his committee:[2]

1. Remember these young adults in prayer, both private and public; see that they are remembered regularly at church services.
2. Keep an accurate, up-to-date mailing list. The serviceman's family is the best source of his current address. This should be checked frequently.
3. Keep mail flowing to them. Learn postal requirements for sending letters and parcels to servicemen. This by itself is a many-faceted subject. It is conveniently laid out in *Mail for Servicemen . . . A Postal Guide for Speeding Service*, an 8-page leaflet available at Post Offices or at the U.S. Government Printing Office, Washington, D.C.   20402.
   Personal letters are welcomed the most. Newsletters and Sunday worship programs, newspaper clippings, notes about high school or college activities, or about anything in which the young person is personally interested should be sent.
4. Use tape recordings. These are inexpensively mailed. Someone in the congregation may have a tape recorder. Red Cross chapters will tape messages without charge, and the USO has a *Living Letters Manual* on community-wide tape recording programs. Messages should be cheery and, as often as possible, should come from the young person's friends and peers.
5. Send suitable periodicals, both religious and secular. Denominational magazines, those on sports or other special interests are appreciated, as are the more general magazines. Try to send these from the local church. It will be work, but a current address can be maintained from this point more easily than from the circulation department of a large magazine. Avoid having your gift copies pile up at some base for months after your GI has left it. (But then again, they may be read by those who follow him! We must look after one another's sons and daughters!) Reasonably current back issues are quite acceptable.
   The LINK, published by the General Commission on Chaplains and Armed Forces Personnel, 122 Maryland Ave., N.W. Wash. D.C. 20002, is an interdenominational monthly designed for servicemen.
6. Send paper-backs. Many a chaplain has written his thanks for reading matter flexible, small in size, and readily pulled from a pocket or bedroll.

[2] cf. *Guidelines to Support U.S. Service Personnel* published by the Office of the Assistant Secretary of Defense, Washington, D.C.   20301. Lists military hospitals in U.S., and other helpful information.

Send them to individual servicemen, to Office of the Chaplain (specify the unit and APO or FPO Number & U.S. Port City); or, Office of the Command Chaplain, HQ. MACV, APO San Francisco, Calif. 96222.

7. Remember birthdays and anniversaries.

8. Give your serviceman a letter of introduction which he can present to churches of his denomination wherever he goes. If possible, write the clergyman of the church nearest his base to inform him of his presence. Addresses of "adjacent" congregations can be obtained from each denomination's military chaplaincy executive. The GI should be encouraged to visit as many different churches as possible during his tour. (Remember that men in basic training have little free time and are unavailable to civilian clergy.)

9. Provide the serviceman going overseas with addresses of English-speaking congregations where he will be. Encourage him to visit indigenous churches also.

10. Make sure the "Welcome" mat is out when he comes home on leave. Be hospitable, but let hospitality be informal and appropriate to youthful interests. Too much "fuss" can become formidable.

11. Churches in large cities can offer Sunday dinner with a private family to visiting servicemen. They can arrange invitations to back-yard cook-outs, picnics, a trip to the beach, an evening at the theater, the concert, the ball park, etc. They can make their invitations known to USO offices or to the senior chaplain at nearby military installations.

12. Keep in touch with the homes, parents, and dependents of servicemen. Be ready to assist them with a pastoral ministry as needed. The importance of this to a distant GI's morale is obvious.

"Happy Boxes"

One imaginative gal kept a whole company of Marines happy:

I sent Don happy boxes. These included powdered, sweetened punch; instant coffee in a plastic container so it won't break or rust; dehydrated soup; chewing gum. I sent enough for the whole platoon, and they had a bubble-gum blowing contest. . . I also included hard candy, plastic-wrapped; some tubes of toothpaste; talcum powder; a small tube of deep-heat rub; bug repellent, but not in an aerosol can; razor blades; soap in bars small enough to be carried in a shirt pocket; lighter flints, but not fluid; a small pocket flashlight; long black shoelaces and black shoe polish; comic books and paperbacks; plastic wrap; and playing cards. I kept the boxes under 5 pounds. (Quoted from the Hackensack, *N.J. Record* 4/13/68)

Do not use vague addresses, i.e. "A serviceman in Vietnam." Gifts *can* be sent to a specific military unit in care of its commanding officer. Before sending anything, the donor is wise to write and ask about specific needs. While over 500,000 GIs are in Vietnam, an equal number are in other parts of the world. They, too, will welcome gifts.

Americans can assist the Vietnamese people through the many military units which work closely with Vietnamese civilians. Checks may be made out to the MACV Chaplain Fund (Civic Action Account) and mailed to: Office of the Staff Chaplain, Headquarters, MACV (CAAP), APO San Francisco, Calif. 96222. Contributors may specify a particular Vietnamese religious charitable institution; when none is specified donations are made to non-sectarian institutions. Again, it is well to write and ask what is needed. GIs all over the world have their favorite civilian aid projects and welcome backing from home.

If a Military Installation Is Near-by

Military installations dot the U.S. landscape and both our coasts. Some are huge, some tiny; some accomodate thousands of people, others the merest handful. Some throb with activity around the clock; others are in "mothballs." Some have been military centers since before the Revolution. Ten generations of experience with servicemen may have induced attitudes which do not change easily. Other bases are brand-new; they and the civilian community may be in a somewhat difficult process of adjustment. Still others are in remote, unpopulated districts. Many are close to metropolitan centers. Small or large, they pump millions of dollars into the civilian economy. They proffer adjacent civilian congregations a challenging opportunity and a valuable resource. A congregation (or a clergyman) can have a wonderful relationship with a near-by base—or a miserable one. The honoring of a few rules can make the difference.

"Ground Rules" for Parish-Installation Relationships

1. The congregation's mission is worship and service to all. Its pastor and people must approach the near-by installation in a spirit of "What can we do to assist you?" Unfortunately, it happens occasionally that a clergyman will appear at the office of a chaplain—or even of the commanding officer—and make demands. "Give me a list of your personnel who belong to my denomination!" Not only will he probably not receive the list, but he will have lost his entree for the future. No

civilian denominational representative may properly behave in preemptory fashion on a military base. Civilian church personnel are admitted to installations as a courtesy; a like courtesy and thoughtfulness should characterize their behavior. Such an attitude will ensure civilian religious leaders of a wholesome, irreproachable basis for their activity. It will help mightily to avert misunderstandings and to reassure understandably skeptical military leaders that this segment of the community is not essentially parasitic. One of the most helpful things a congregation can do is to find adequate, inexpensive housing for families in the lower pay grades.

2. Civilian church planning must be flexible. Not only do commanding officers, chaplains, and other personnel come and go, but the installations themselves rise and wane. Sometimes they disappear. No denomination should base construction or continuance of facilities upon anticipation of military contributions.

3. Some commanding officers are religious men, and some are not. Some chaplains are zealous for the on-base religious program and resent what they deem to be "competition" or "interference" from outside the installation. Others work harmoniously with local churches. A base may never have had assigned to it a chaplain of persuasion "X"; it may have employed a clergyman of that faith as a civilian auxiliary. Suddenly, that clergyman's military counterpart reports to the base, and the civilian loses his job! It would be strange if there were not a bit of tension between these two clerics of the same denomination. Given the transiency of military personnel, the fluctuations of command policy, the sometimes checkered pattern of base-community relationships, and the vagaries of human nature, it is not surprising that a civilian clergyman's entree and sense of welcome on an installation exhibit marked "ups and downs." Inherently, the "system" and human diversity are responsible.

4. On his first visit to a military base a civilian clergyman should pay a courtesy call on its senior chaplain, the "channel" through which he can have official access to the installation. The senior chaplain—or his subordinate—can then present the visitor to the commanding officer. Neatness, heavily stressed in military life, is noted and welcomed in civilian callers. Observe automobile speed limits scrupulously. The military is adamant about this and expects visitors to comply. Should one pass marching troops in the roadway, the speed limit is 5 mph. In summary: go through channels. Don't demand special privileges. Ask how you can help.

A Quiz on That Base Near Your Church

What sort of an installation is it? What is its "mission"? Who is its commanding officer? Does he have a staff? How many chaplains are there? What is the recent history of base-community relationships? What are considered by the military to be problem areas? By civilians? Is there a civilian advisory committee to the installation commander? What are housing patterns? How many civilians does the base employ? How much money does it pump into the local economy? To what extent does the community, including the churches, really accept these transient military strangers? Does the church welcome them on boards, vestries, choirs, church school staffs, etc.? Does the ministerial association invite the chaplains to its meetings? Are these ever held on the base?

The Community Can Honor the Installation Near It

By Presidential proclamation, the third Saturday in May is designated "Armed Forces Day." Military bases usually hold "open house" and have special programs for the public. The weekend offers congregations in the vicinity an opportunity to honor their military neighbors.

Full and solemn observance of Memorial Day and Veterans Day (November 11th) with appropriate prayers, music, and addresses is important to the spiritual health of the community. Here the churches can provide unique leadership.

	E-1	E-2	E-3	E-4	E-5	E-6	E-7	E-8	E-9	W-1	W-2
NAVY & COAST GUARD	SEAMAN RECRUIT	SEAMAN APPRENTICE	SEAMAN	PETTY OFFICER THIRD CLASS	PETTY OFFICER SECOND CLASS	PETTY OFFICER FIRST CLASS	CHIEF PETTY OFFICER	SENIOR CHIEF PETTY OFFICER	MASTER CHIEF PETTY OFFICER	WARRANT OFFICER W 1	CHIEF WARRANT OFFICER W 2
MARINES	PRIVATE	PRIVATE FIRST CLASS	LANCE CORPORAL	CORPORAL	SERGEANT	STAFF SERGEANT	GUNNERY SERGEANT	1ST SGT / MSGT	SGT MAJOR / MGY SGT	WARRANT OFFICER W 1	CHIEF WARRANT OFFICER W 2
ARMY	PRIVATE	PRIVATE	PRIVATE FIRST CLASS	CORPORAL / SPECIALIST 4	SERGEANT / SPECIALIST 5	STAFF SERGEANT / SPECIALIST 6	SERGEANT FIRST CLASS / SPECIALIST 7	1ST SGT / MSGT	SERGEANT MAJOR	WARRANT OFFICER W 1	CHIEF WARRANT OFFICER W 2
AIR FORCE	AIRMAN	AIRMAN THIRD CLASS	AIRMAN SECOND CLASS	AIRMAN FIRST CLASS	STAFF SERGEANT	TECHNICAL SERGEANT	MASTER SERGEANT	SENIOR MASTER SERGEANT	CHIEF MASTER SERGEANT	WARRANT OFFICER W 1	CHIEF WARRANT OFFICER W 2

ENLISTED — WAR

Coast Guard insignia are the same as Navy except that a shield is worn on sleeve and shoulder boards in lieu of a star.

64

U. S. ARMED FORCES

W-3	W-4	O-1	O-2	O-3	O-4	O-5	O-6	O-7	O-7 O-8	O-9	O-10	Special
SILVER BLUE	SILVER BLUE	GOLD	SILVER	SILVER	GOLD	SILVER	SILVER	SILVER	SILVER	SILVER	SILVER	SILVER
CHIEF WARRANT OFFICER W 3	CHIEF WARRANT OFFICER W 4	ENSIGN	LIEUTENANT JUNIOR GRADE	LIEUTENANT	LIEUTENANT COMMANDER	COMMANDER	CAPTAIN	COMMODORE	REAR ADMIRAL	VICE ADMIRAL	ADMIRAL	FLEET ADMIRAL
SILVER SCARLET	SILVER SCARLET	GOLD	SILVER	SILVER	GOLD	SILVER	SILVER	SILVER	SILVER	SILVER	SILVER	
CHIEF WARRANT OFFICER W 3	CHIEF WARRANT OFFICER W 4	SECOND LIEUTENANT	FIRST LIEUTENANT	CAPTAIN	MAJOR	LIEUTENANT COLONEL	COLONEL	BRIGADIER GENERAL	MAJOR GENERAL	LIEUTENANT GENERAL	GENERAL	
SILVER BROWN	SILVER BROWN	GOLD	SILVER	SILVER	GOLD	SILVER	SILVER	SILVER	SILVER	SILVER	SILVER	SILVER
CHIEF WARRANT OFFICER W 3	CHIEF WARRANT OFFICER W 4	SECOND LIEUTENANT	FIRST LIEUTENANT	CAPTAIN	MAJOR	LIEUTENANT COLONEL	COLONEL	BRIGADIER GENERAL	MAJOR GENERAL	LIEUTENANT GENERAL	GENERAL	GENERAL OF THE ARMY
SILVER SKY BLUE	SILVER SKY BLUE	GOLD	SILVER	SILVER	GOLD	SILVER	SILVER	SILVER	SILVER	SILVER	SILVER	SILVER
CHIEF WARRANT OFFICER W 3	CHIEF WARRANT OFFICER W 4	SECOND LIEUTENANT	LIEUTENANT	CAPTAIN	MAJOR	LIEUTENANT COLONEL	COLONEL	BRIGADIER GENERAL	MAJOR GENERAL	LIEUTENANT GENERAL	GENERAL	GENERAL OF THE AIR FORCE

65

Chapter 9

The Military Chaplaincy

THE military chaplaincy is the largest of the federal chaplaincies. Its roots extend back certainly to seventeenth-century Britain. In 1756 during the French and Indian War, Col. George Washington requested a chaplain for his troops.[1] After the outbreak of the Revolution the Continental Congress took formal action to create a military chaplaincy for its troops. The date: July 29, 1775. Naval chaplains were authorized on the 28th of November. Like the great majority of colonists, the chaplains were nearly all Protestant. A Roman Catholic priest, Fr. Lotbinier, was appointed to a Canadian regiment on January 26, 1776. Clergymen of the Episcopal Church served on opposing sides. Owing their ordination to the Established Church in Britain and having sworn allegiance to the Crown, many of them left their parishes and removed to Canada or England. A number sided with the "Rebels." The war decimated their church.

After the Revolution the chaplaincy fell into obscurity. A handful of chaplains served in the War of 1812; in the 1820's the Secretary of the Navy issued a series of regulations concerning the qualifications of chaplains. Funds for twenty chaplains for army posts were authorized in 1838. In 1852-3 the first challenges of the constitutionality of the chaplaincy appeared and continued to the eve of the Civil War. The judiciary committees of Congress repeatedly affirmed the legality of existing arrangements. Their rulings are still milestones in the history of chaplaincy litigation.[1]

In the Civil War some 2,300 chaplains served with the Union Forces. A large number wore Confederate grey.[2] A marked expansion, both in numbers and in the development of regulations, occurred in response to the demands of the War. Yet, within a dozen years of Appomattox, the status of the chaplain had reverted to that of "school teacher-librarian" on army posts. In 1901 Congress laid down the foundations of the modern chaplaincy by calling for chaplains who were qualified and formally endorsed by their denominations. The system became normative in 1913.

America's entry into World War I produced an interdenominational agency on the chaplaincy. The General Committee on Army and Navy Chaplains was formed on March 28, 1917 at the request of Newton D. Baker, Secretary of War. The number of Army chaplains rose from 176 to 2,300 and in the Navy from 24 to 203.[3] The first Chief of Chaplains was Charles Henry Brent, an Episcopal bishop. General Pershing made the appointment. A key aspect of the work of these years was the development of criteria for the endorsement of chaplains. The committee insisted upon a college degree and, if possible, seminary training. This had not been part of the government's stipulation in 1917. It is now the backbone of official requirements.

The Committee was instrumental also in the establishment of a chaplain's school at Fort Monroe, Virginia. After several shifts of location, it went into obscurity until 1942 when it was hastily reestablished at Fort Benjamin Harrison, Indiana. Most of the World War II chaplains, however, were trained at Harvard University. Today the Army Chaplain School flourishes at Fort Hamilton, Brooklyn, N.Y. Naval chaplains are trained at Newport, R. I., while the Air Force Chaplain's School is at Maxwell Air Force Base, Alabama.

The twenties and thirties were difficult years for the chaplaincy. There was renewed pressure to "civilianize" it. Support from the denominations did not waver, however, and when the storm of World War II burst upon the nation, the needed ecclesiastical machinery was at hand. Over 8,000 clergymen served as Army chaplains; 3,000 more served in the Navy. Seventy-eight were killed on active duty, and 264 were wounded. Nearly 2,400 were decorated for extraordinary heroism. Thousands of congregations sent their pastors off to minister to the 12,000,000 men and women in uniform. These chaplains did their job and did it well. The four who died together on the *Dorchester* symbolize their devotion.

Continuance of world tension halted and then reversed the demobilization begun after the defeat of Japan. An international force, fighting under the flag of the United Nations, spent three years in Korea. Again, chaplains were in the field and aboard the ships. Since the Korean War the Armed Forces have not had fewer than 2,500 chaplains on active duty. Development of the chaplaincy has continued as the Armed Forces have responded to the swiftly changing world situation. The Air Force obtained its own chaplaincy in 1949.

At the end of 1967 Army, Navy, and Air Force had a combined active roster of 4,100 chaplains representing about fifty denominations. Over 500 of these men are in Vietnam.

No longer a forgotten man among clergymen, the chaplain is a member of a large corps of professional specialists. Sensitive issues pertaining to the chaplaincy are still very much alive,[4] yet there is no question about the ability of American clergymen to serve with great distinction in the uniform of the United States.

The Chaplain's Job

The chaplain is a staff assistant to the commanding officer.[5] He is fully a member of the Armed Forces, though subject to powerful controls from his denomination. He goes with the troops, is paid by the military, and is fully subject to its orders. A volunteer, he enlists for a three-year tour, or sometimes, as in the case of Jewish rabbis, for two years. He has an officer's privileges and responsibilities, may win promotion all the way to flag rank, serve twenty or more years, and qualify for a liberal government pension.

Nevertheless, he remains a clergyman in uniform, on loan from his denomination. His acceptability as a chaplain is contingent upon his continuance in good standing within it. The withdrawal of its ecclesiastical endorsement brings immediate separation from duty. Apart from variations inherent in his branch of service, the role of the chaplain is the same throughout the Forces. First of all, he is a man of God, duly ordained, an approved and experienced representative of his denomination. He is not asked to compromise his religious convictions or his practice in worship. A religious and spiritual leader in the military community, his duties are "analogous to those performed by clergymen in civilian life." [6] As a specialist in the field of religious guidance, he is "advisor to the commanding officer on all matters pertaining to the moral, spiritual, and religious welfare of personnel." [7]

He conducts divine service in accordance with the customs, and traditions of his own church. He provides religious services and other ministrations for those of other faiths; his pastoral concern extends to all in his unit. He makes provision for the religious needs of all and will bring in auxiliary personnel when necessary. Should it prove impracticable by reason of distance, size, or isolation to provide the services of a suitable clergyman, the chaplain will arrange coverage by a lay assistant.

The chaplain must live and work in the closest proximity to people of all religious persuasions—or none. Exposure to such a variety of religious experience challenges him to re-examine his own position in the light of fresh evidence; it generates new respect for other viewpoints. "Cooperation without compromise" is considerably more than a pious slogan.

The "padre" is a full-time counselor. His "ministry of listening" is one of his most important functions. The Services give many chaplains post-graduate training in counseling. Some obtain graduate degrees from civilian universities. Much attention is paid to career management. Subject, of course, to the needs of the service, he is moved to new assignments, usually at two or three year intervals. He is constantly watched and tested. In due time an assignment overseas or to sea duty materializes. In hardship or combat zones his family will have to remain at home. Such separations are part of the life he shares with the troops. His wife must be able to "carry on"—and she should share in her husband's initial decision for the chaplaincy.

The chaplain may direct or be on the staff of a large, well-equipped chapel with a "parish program" much like those at home. He may preach to great congregations or to the merest handful of worshipers. He may have to conduct services in the field with make-shift equipment. All outward props may be stripped away; his training and his own inner resources must serve to fortify his men. He may find himself "circuit riding" between widely separated units and using any transportation available, whether "holy helo," jeep, "high line," or "shank's mare." He may tend wounded men under fire, hold a dying man in his arms, or pray with airmen beside a giant plane. He may serve in a military hospital or prison, jump with paratroopers, "hit the beach" with marines, or shuffle papers in an office. On foreign shores he may be occupied with humanitarian projects. He will teach classes and attend them. Besides his weekly and daily services, he will officiate at baptisms, weddings, and funerals. He will be detailed to comfort the families of casualties. Dependents will claim much of his time.

Administration of the Chaplaincy

The chaplaincy necessarily involves a partnership between the religious bodies of the United States and the federal military authorities. By law the direct supervision of the chaplains is entrusted to the respective Chiefs of Chaplains. The Chiefs depend on a duly appointed executive in each denomination to endorse officially chaplain candidates. For certain denominations a certifying function is provided by the General Commission on Chaplains and Armed Forces Personnel in Washington, D.C.[8]

A civilian clergyman considering the chaplaincy should apply to his denomination's "endorsing executive." Subsequently, a separate application is made via the nearest recruiting station. The candidate must meet the criteria announced by his own denomination as well as those of the Chief's office. A security check is involved. Processing normally takes three to six months. In no case should a civilian clergyman applying for extended active duty resign from his cure until he has received official orders to report.

Local military recruiting offices can assist initially, but inquiries and applications for full-time active duty should be addressed as follows:

ARMY   Chief of Chaplains
       Department of the Army
       Washington, D.C. 20315

NAVY   Chief of Chaplains (J123)
       Bureau of Naval Personnel
       Navy Department
       Washington, D.C.   20370

AIR FORCE   Chief of Chaplains
       Field Extension
       Randolph Air Force Base, Texas   78148

At present, the chaplain candidate must be:

1. A male citizen of the United States or one who lawfully entered the United States for permanent residence.
2. Under 33 years of age at the time of appointment. Occasionally, waivers are granted.
3. Physically qualified.
4. In possession of 120 semester-hour credits of undergraduate study at an accredited college or university and a minimum of 90 semester-hour credits of study performed in a recognized theological school, or equivalent credits in the fields of religion and the social sciences performed in an accredited university or other graduate school.
5. A regularly ordained clergyman endorsed for the Chaplaincy by a recognized religious denomination.
6. Actively engaged in the ministry as his principal vocation in life.
7. Able to receive a favorable security clearance.

Other Programs

1. **Inactive Reserve.** Each Service has a Reserve program for chaplains not on active duty. The requirements are similar to those for full-time chaplains. Information may be obtained from Reserve units, recruiting offices, the Chiefs of Chaplains, and Endorsing Executives. Reserve

chaplains are called to active duty only in time of national emergency or in the mobilizing of certain units by Presidential Order. Applications should be submitted through the local Reserve or National Guard unit. Participation in a Reserve program may enable a clergyman to build up retirement credit points so that he may eventually qualify for a government pension.

2. **Seminarian Programs.** Each Service also invites seminarians to prepare for the chaplaincy. This involves summer attendance at Chaplain's School. He is commissioned a Reserve (inactive) Second Lieutenant (Army and Air Force) or an Ensign in the Navy. It should be noted that most denominations require a term of experience in the civilian ministry before they will grant an ecclesiastical endorsement. The seminarian programs also add to pay and retirement credits.

3. **The Lay Ministry.** The Armed Forces provide laymen with significant opportunities for a religious ministry. Many military units are too small to have a chaplain. The chaplain's assistant, long a familiar figure around military chapels, now receives training as a specialist. The Navy has a Lay Leader program which helps to provide a ministry aboard vessels such as Polaris submarines which do not normally carry a chaplain. Lay Leaders may be officers or enlisted men and work under the chaplain's supervision. These lay ministries keep the Services abreast of the increasing stress on lay leadership in civilian churches.

4. **The Civil Air Patrol.** The Civil Air Patrol is a "federally chartered volunteer organization with status as an auxiliary of the United States Air Force." [9] Organized on 1 December, 1941, it numbers approximately 76,000 members in over 2,000 squadrons in the U.S. and includes 1,200 chaplains of all faiths.[10] CAP chaplains are endorsed by their denominations through the normal channels, but requirements are not as stringent as for military chaplains. There is no obligation which would bring a CAP chaplain to active duty in the Air Force.

Address inquiries to: The National Chaplain, National Headquarters
The Civil Air Patrol
Maxwell Air Force Base, Alabama   36112

5. **The Veterans Administration Chaplaincy.** Endorsing executives also pass upon the applications of clergymen for admission as full and

part-time chaplains in Veterans Administration hospitals. Though its origins go back to 1865,[11] the present VA Chaplaincy dates from 1945. This is now a major, federally operated ministry among civilians. It involves over 275 full-time and 440 part-time chaplains in 171 hospitals across the country. For further information, write:

The Director, Chaplain Service
Veterans Administration Central Office
Washington, D.C.   20420

NOTES

1. cf. Art. *The Chaplaincy in American Public Life* by Eugene F. Klug in THE CHAPLAIN, Feb., 1966, pp. 15-45.
2. cf. Art. *A Confederate Chaplain's Diary* by Calvin D. Jarret, THE CHAPLAIN, March-April, 1967, pp. 16-20.
3. cf. Art. *A Half-Century in Behalf of the Chaplaincy* by Spencer D. McQueen, THE CHAPLAIN, May-June, 1967, pp. 4-42.
4. cf. Art. *The Constitutionality of the U.S. Military Chaplaincy* by Klaus J. Herrmann, THE CHAPLAIN, June, 1965, pp. 32-47.
5. *Department of the Army Field Manual,* "The Chaplain", FM 16-5, Aug. 1964, p. 3.
   Bureau of Naval Personnel, *Chaplain's Manual* (NAVPERS 15664-B, March, 1959, Sect. 1200, p. 2)
   Department of the Air Force, AFR 165-3, 24 Sept. 1953, p. 1; *The Air Force Chaplain,* AFM 165-3, June, 1956.
6. Dept. of the Army, "The Chaplain", op. cit., p. 1
7. Dept. of the Air Force, *The Air Force Chaplain, op. cit.* p. 15
8. The General Commission is comprised of 36 Protestant denominations and under the laws of the District of Columbia forms a permanent conference on the chaplaincy. It is not organic to, but works cooperatively with the National Council of Churches, the American Bible Society, American Leprosy Missions, Inc. and similar agencies. Lutheran, Southern Baptist, and other religious groups contribute to the Commission's support. Chaplaincy executives of these bodies are consultants to the Commission. Its address: 122 Maryland Ave., N.E., Washington, D.C.   20002.
9. *The Challenge of the Chaplaincy,* CAP Pamphlet 18 (Rev'd 7/63).
10. cf. Art. *The Chaplaincy in the Civil Air Patrol* by Victor H. Schroeder, THE CHAPLAIN, Jan.-Feb., 1967, pp. 38-40.
11. cf. Art. *Chaplain Service in Veterans Administration Hospitals* by Morris A. Sandhaus, THE CHAPLAIN, June, 1963, pp. 40-47.

Chapter 10

Necessities of Military Life

U NFORTUNATELY, society cannot yet function without coercion. Laws must be enforced and life and property protected. To this end we employ policemen. With international society the situation is even more primitive. No nation has freely concluded that it can feel entirely secure without a military force—and atomic weapons threaten every nation. Men of sense and goodwill, particularly those who stand in the Judaeo-Christian tradition, seek desperately to lead mankind away from the resort to violence. But their day has not yet come. Coercion remains a social necessity, rooted in the harsher realities of human nature.

This chapter discusses the characteristics of a military force which enable it to perform its coercive function. These are: motivation; regimentation; training, discipline, and drill; education; weapons, and mobility. They are constants on the military scene. All armies exhibit them. An effective force is impossible without them. Furthermore, they reflect the society in which they appear. Just as ours is a mass society dominated by technology, modern military forces are mass entities wedded to technology. However ominous it may sound, many of the differences between civilian and military life are fading. Mercifully, the trend is far from complete, but it is there. City life requires a not insubstantial measure of regimentation. The greater the earth's population density, the more this will be true.

Motivation

War is brutal, hellish, insane. That men should resort to it suggests how short has been their advance toward civilization. Yet, they still fight. What drives them to it? The answer requires a treatise on human nature. The present purpose, however, is to stress the factor of motivation as a first "necessity" of military life. An army must have at least a rudimentary understanding of why it fights. It cannot finally be driven or paid enough to make it loyal. It must, in a word, consent. There are some interesting comments about this in Henry Felsen's book, *To My Son in Uniform:*

What is at stake is not winning some kind of shooting game, but the welfare of our country, and doing what is best for our country.

. . . It is because each army has been convinced that it alone fights for truth, justice, and freedom that the fight is so bitter.

Every army marches off to war with blessings and cheers and a beloved homeland to defend and in the pockets of the slain on both sides, the letters and pictures are heartbreakingly the same. . . What is true in battle is true at home.

The majority of those who oppose the war do so because they honestly believe war is against the best interests of the United States. . . And a majority of those who favor the war honestly believe that it is the best way to safeguard our country and its freedoms. . .

Despite much pressure for an official patriotism, . . . we still allow our citizens to speak out. Freedom of speech and assembly exists. Our government protects its critics. And as long as this continues, you have a country to fight for. As long as this is what you fight for, you deserve to be its citizen.

Look at it this way: You are fighting as now you must, to preserve freedom and democracy in the world. If you lose, your fellow citizens—including the anti-war citizens—lose their freedoms as well.
    Yet, while you fight for them abroad in your way, they are fighting some of your battles here at home—for the freedom of any citizen to speak up, to disagree, to hold unpopular opinions, to act according to his conscience. And if they lose their freedom to do this, your free citizenship goes down the drain.[1]

Regimentation—To Protect Life and Health
    In the Armed Forces regimentation is "mass life in a military context." Large numbers of men live in close physical proximity under relatively primitive conditions. They share the same toilets, wash-

[1] N.Y. Dodd, Mead & Co. 1966. 125 pp. cf. pp. 53-61.

rooms, sleeping quarters, and mess halls. There is little privacy. The implications for public health are serious. The attention paid to cleanliness and "spit and polish" is not capricious. Regulations are stringently enforced because health and safety require it.

The need to subordinate the interests of the individual to the welfare of a larger unit—the squad, platoon, company, etc.—appears to the outsider to lead to de-personalization. In point of fact, inside a military unit all privates and most noncommissioned officers are known by name, not by number or rank. This is quite different from the growing anonymity of civilian life. The soldier is trained to commit himself to his unit because his life may depend upon it. The success of a patrol and its safe return from enemy territory can pivot on the attention each man has paid to his gear and to compliance with orders. Attention to detail and the submergence of personal whim are of life and death importance; they are inculcated at every level of military training. There is no avoiding them, and none is permitted. On the other hand, the individual's importance to the unit is fully recognized and gets conscientious attention.

Training, Discipline, and Drill

The only avenue to a state of constant readiness is practice and the continuous up-dating of equipment and technique. The unprepared army is useless. Drill, exercises, maneuvers, and testing are essential features of military life. There is heavy emphasis upon proficiency. Performance is a key to promotion. The Armed Forces have pioneered in the development of large scale testing and evaluation techniques.

Early Training*

The Armed Forces purposely shock their initial trainees into military life. They are treated firmly with little to say and lots to do. They are kept physically and mentally occupied all day long from early reveille to late taps. They are ordered around, not listened to, depreciated, and physically exhausted.

This approach resulted from an extensive psychological testing program during and after WW II. No aspect of military instruction has received more scrupulous attention. It purposely counters the revolt by which a young man reacts and reduces the homesickness

* For portions of this and the following section I am indebted to Captain G. H. Weller, Legal Officer, Third Coast Guard District.

which can result from idleness. The generally permissive atmosphere of a teen's civilian life is shocked out of him by minutely organizing his day and demanding his prompt obedience to seniors, particularly his drill instructor or his platoon commander.

The purpose is to sever his ties to his former surroundings and to develop a pride and loyalty to his new society. And psychologically this begins to happen. Gradually there develops a rapport between the members of the platoon which transcends all other loyalties. In effect and in fact the teen becomes a "marine," a "sailor," a "soldier," an "airman," or a "coast guardsman" with a deep sense of pride in himself, his unit, and his service. These initial training programs have been carefully planned to produce this result. At first they seem harsh and unreasonable, but they do work. Since the men are "short-timers," they must be trained rapidly.

Particular care is paid to the selection and training of drill instructors. Chosen for their intelligence and leadership qualifications, they undergo four-to-six-week courses of intensive instruction.

Recruits learn physical conditioning, rifle marksmanship, the school or squad or fire team, hand-to-hand combat, personal hygiene, marching, first aid, survival in the field, elementary tactics, and general military indoctrination. The Navy "boot" also learns the elements of seamanship and fire-fighting. Marine Corps "boot" training is the toughest, physically and psychologically, of all the services.

BASIC TRAINING CENTERS

ARMY (8 weeks)

Fort Dix, N.J., 08640

Fort Campbell, Ky., 42223

Fort Knox, Ky., 40121

Fort Jackson, S.C., 29207

Fort Gordon, Ga., 30905

Fort Benning, Ga., 31905

Fort Polk, La., 71459

Fort Bliss, Tex., 79906

Fort Leonard Wood, Mo., 65475

Fort Ord, Calif., 93941

Fort Lewis, Wash., 98433

Fort Bragg, N.C., 28307

AIR FORCE (8 weeks)

Lackland AFB, Texas 78236

MARINE CORPS (8 weeks)

Parris Island, S.C., 29905

San Diego, Calif., 92133

NAVY (10 weeks)

Great Lakes, Ill., 60088

San Diego, Calif., 92133

Orlando, Fla., (in 1970)

COAST GUARD (8 weeks)

Cape May, N.J., 08212

Alameda, Calif., 94501

FILMS ON BASIC TRAINING are also available for public showing. Detailed instructions for obtaining them are given in the Film section of the Bibliography, Chapter 16. The following are recommended. All are cleared for TV use.

ARMY
The Men from the Boys, No. RF-21, Color, 52 min. 1967. Portrays eight weeks in the life of a group of young men from their induction through basic training. The film shows the men being moulded into a well-trained unit and ends as each receives his assignment.

AIR FORCE
Letter from an Airman, SFP 1211, Color, 17 min. 1964. Depicts an airman's thoughts as he writes his brother about Air Force basic training. Shows trainee life from induction to special assignment. Cites the specialized training that prepares the airman for a rewarding career.

NAVY
Ready for Sea, MN-7445, B/W, 15 min. 1952. A young sailor approaching his first ship wonders, "Am I ready for Sea?" The film flashes back to his reporting for recruit training in San Diego with other bewildered "boots." Shows him experiencing Navy drill and discipline, studying Navy traditions and courtesies and making liberty expeditions.

MARINE CORPS
The First Eighty Days, MH 10143, Color, 18 min. 1967. Shows the first eighty days of recruit training at Parris Island, S.C.

COAST GUARD
Shine the Boot, No. 28, Color, 14 min. 1956. Depicts recruit training, associations and other activities of a young man from time of enlistment to initial duty assignment.

Later Training—Discipline Relaxes
Following "basic" training there is a greater freedom and a more relaxed relationship between personnel. Seldom are orders given with the idea of blind obedience. Intelligence is expected in the giving or the execution of orders. Except in the throes of battle or drills, reasons for orders are generally explained and latitude is given in their means of execution. There is a gradual growth of understanding as to the roles played by each person and less of a need to order anyone to do anything. Rather, jobs are performed by men who know what to do and how to do it. Occasionally a martinet is found, but he is generally

an insecure man, much in the minority.

The one thing a professional military man cannot tolerate is direct disobedience of an order, but seldom does such a situation arise and seldom is there an occasion for direct disobedience.

As with any other large organization, government or civilian, the personalities of the individuals involved determine the success or pleasantness of the jobs being done. In the military one or the other of clashing personalities will probably be transferred, so the specter of working for an unpleasant boss for years, which can sometimes accompany a civilian job, is not present.

Career military men understand that most volunteers and draftees are in for only one tour. They are tolerant of and usually participants in "bull sessions" on the Armed Forces, politics, etc., as long as they are not personally attacked. Opinions are respected, opinions of a wide spectrum, but not from the man who always complains but never does his job. A young man's opinion is respected to the degree that the young man is respected—and he is respected to the extent that he puts his best into his job.

Education

To complete his qualification for duty a man may go to schools of many kinds. As military hardware grows more sophisticated and as personnel require greater political and social sensitivity, educational levels rise. An ever-larger proportion of servicemen receive full or partial college training. The maintenance of a large, essentially civilian army means a high rate of turnover and a correspondingly high training expense. Probably one-fifth of the average serviceman's career is spent in school. Frequently he acquires skills which fit him for high-paying jobs in later civilian life. Chapter Three discusses the Armed Forces as the world's largest educational organization.

Weapons

An army's strength is heavily in its "firepower"—in its possession of and ability to use weapons. These today are awesome in their variety and capability. But the soldier's basic weapon remains the rifle. The recruit begins at once to learn how to use and maintain it. He will come to know its every part and be able to assemble it blindfolded. He learns to clean and protect it, handle it safely, and to respect it. Later, he may learn to use other weapons in the military arsenal. He may spend weeks in school becoming a specialist in explosives and the direction of firepower.

Mobility

The final military "necessity" is mobility. The speed with which coercion can be applied is a crucial political consideration. To get there "fastest with the mostest" confers a commanding advantage, if not victory itself—although in the context of nuclear weapons this doctrine breaks down. The non-nuclear, six-day Egyptian-Israeli war of June, 1968 illustrates the general statement. Nuclear warfare aside, any military force which can move large numbers of men and much equipment rapidly across almost any distance will be formidable. While the soldier does a lot of waiting, he learns to move—on short notice.

Chapter 11

The Experiences of Military Life

UNIVERSAL experiences await the serviceman: accomplishment, satisfaction, growth, schooling, comradeship, travel, loneliness, boredom, hardship, discipline, temptations, coarseness and brutality, weariness, sickness, pain, sorrow, hostility, fear, and, possibly, combat and death. The milieu imparts poignance, trauma, memorableness, and intensity to experience, yet life is essentially the same, wherever encountered. It is impossible to describe the experience of the soldier, or, for that matter, of the student or the young businessman. In these few pages we shall examine the more typical military experiences and then refer the reader to classic books which powerfully depict the life of the fighting man. Hundreds are available. The following sections arbitrarily set certain aspects of military life in a "positive" and "negative" juxtaposition, although the "goodness" or "badness" of our experience depends in large measure upon ourselves—and upon the passage of time.

Accomplishment, Satisfaction, and Growth vs.
Frustration, Dissatisfaction, and Stagnation

The Armed Forces offer a young man important satisfactions and accomplishments. He can grow physically, mentally, and spiritually. Military service is a unique testing ground. Its equality is pitiless and unparalleled. Family, culture, religion, wealth, education, and station make no difference. A lad is on his own. Nobody saves him from the consequences of his actions. He is placed among his peers in the most elemental circumstances and tested to see of what stuff he is made. In barracks and aboard ship he lives with men of all types—coarse and refined, brutish and sensitive, rich and poor, intelligent and stupid. He need not like them all, but he must work with them and share in a common life. There is value in this. To win acceptance on the basis of performance alone is one of life's deep satisfactions. The Services make maximum demands, but they also reward performance. The hard-won corporal's stripes mean vastly more than a miniscule pay raise. And there is no escape from having to "deliver the goods."

Military service is an opportunity to participate in a special way in the affairs of one's time. No man wisely seeks to escape the common experience of his age. The child's question, "Where were you during the War, Daddy?" implies an expectation that Daddy was occupied with something relevant. When the rest of society is caught up in momentous events, one loses something if one has to say, "I had no part in them."

To learn to function as a member of a team with full acceptance of personal accountability to its other members; to win such mastery over self that one can keep going while aching to quit; to be able to obey orders and accept discipline; to know that one is reliable—these are major accomplishments. They retain their value in civilian life. Thus, military service has a refining, purging effect. It can conduct one swiftly into adulthood.

Also, it offers a breathing period within which to read and think and talk. The give-and-take with one's peers in totally new surroundings is an invigorating experience. Exposure to the harsher side of life yields insights which come slowly to civilians. In the service one learns that life is a succession of examinations. The need to stay abreast of political and technological developments is eventually felt by every serviceman. He must learn new skills, drill, and keep up. Such pressure has enduring relevance.

But on the Other Hand . . .

One encounters much that seems stupid and wasteful. This is inevitable in an authoritarian society. An army offers little scope for individual creativity and frowns on the "eager beaver." It expects both general and private to obey lawful orders. It goes "by the book." Yet, the presence of the American citizen-soldier has always meant a saving element of common sense.

The soldier's life does not alter over the centuries because military necessity does not change. Armies remain authoritarian entities, issuing regulations by the ream and pin-pointing responsibility. They are ruthless levelers of men, yet they require separation by rank (though now this is more social than functional). All this frustrates many intelligent, imaginative spirits. The deepest frustration of all proceeds from the frightful inconsistencies, the awful necessities into which warfare can draw men.

81

Military life is full of minor annoyances. Griping is a way of life. Under the provocations of elbow-to-elbow living, physical discomfort, institutional cooking, protocol, spit and polish, and a hundred other irritants, no wonder GIs complain! When men are thrown together by command rather than by preference, there is bound to be rasping; it is human nature to gripe, and in the Armed Forces human nature is laid bare.

There can be stagnation. It may involve merely a brief interruption of a civilian career—in most cases an unexpectedly profitable interruption—but still a period of "marking time." Or, it may be that years spent within the authoritarian military framework can have induced such a serious stagnation of spirit and enterprise that prospect of a return to a freer system creates anxieties. The security of governmentally guaranteed food, medical care, housing, commissary privilege, and other benefits can dull the competitive edge.

Comradeship and Loneliness

Military service can produce lasting friendships. Many a GI has returned to civilian life with comradeships he will treasure for the rest of his days. The Services form an enormous family; its members look after one another. Despite many points of similarity, there are differences between servicemen and civilians. The civilian is not under orders. In a crowd of civilians he can be utterly alone. In the same crowd two Marines are not alone. Everywhere the families of servicemen cluster together. This sense of comradeship is a distinctive mark of military life.

But Then Again . . .

There is loneliness. The recruit or draftee may be homesick. The sentry walking a post or keeping watch in a hole in the ground on a winter night is alone with the unknown. "Waiting wives" and their children ache with the pain of separation. The "old man," with eagles or stars on his collar and responsibility for men's lives and for public property on his shoulders, knows the loneliness of command. Many assignments are to isolated outposts; there is no place to go and little to do but watch and wait. Quite different is the loneliness of the recruiting sergeant. Alone in a sea of civilians, he longs for his own milieu. Thus, loneliness in military service has universal overtones: those associated with an irretrievable past, with fear of the unknown, with anxiety for loved ones, with inability to share a burden, with removal from human company, and with the stranger's lot. The Services try valiantly to counter these with many types of off-duty programs. However, there is a solitariness in life that no one can escape. Every soul comes to it. To this elemental human experience religion speaks with consoling power.

High Adventure and Abysmal Tedium

"Join the Navy and See the World!" "Get on the Aero-Space Team!" "It's a Man's Army!" The Armed Forces have substituted the blandishments of Madison Avenue for the tactics of the press gang. Yet, when the extravagant claims have been scaled down the result is not zero. There is adventure and excitement in military service which are simply not available elsewhere. To protest that the posters are a damnable misrepresentation of war's hideousness is to miss the point. Furthermore, the charge that either the Government or its Armed Forces whitewash the horribleness of war is false. Both take their responsibilities much too seriously. They could not otherwise face the public. Moreover, to be in mortal danger is no indifferent, unexciting matter. To whatever extent military service is dangerous it is to that extent exciting. In taking a submarine into the depths, in marching out with a unit of fighting men, in driving a darkened truck down a strange road at night, in manning a ship in rough seas, in flying planes of all types, in struggling to function under adverse conditions there can be great exhilaration. That there can also be misery is not denied; that there is tedium we shall see presently; but that there is drama and suspense in these dangerous activities cannot be gainsaid. Throughout history the human spirit has responded to danger's magnetism. In military service, as elsewhere, the excitement of the contest is a basic human experience. Though they may exaggerate, the recruiting posters reflect genuine experience. They strike a responsive chord.

But Let's Face It . . .

Military life is notorious for its tedium. Every serviceman knows what it is to "hurry up and wait." An army marches only "under orders," and until these arrive it "marks time." For every man in combat there may be fifty in the supply line. Mighty engines of war go largely unused. Moored to a pier, parked in long rows, they wait, wait, wait. There is drill, repetition, and make-work. The business of government is conducted primarily by peaceful means. Military forces are stand-by

83

instrumentalities. Maneuvers help keep them in a state of readiness, but these are not the real thing. General and private alike grow bored. They grouse and try to out-guess their superiors. Excitement and tedium coexist everywhere in life, but nowhere are they as memorable as in military service.

Crisis: Opportunity and Danger

Young adulthood is a time of crisis. It presents new opportunities and new dangers. The young soldier faces many interesting possibilities and very real hazards. He can travel widely, see how other people live, and expose himself to outlooks both novel and strange. He can taste cultures other than his own and learn to appreciate the richness of the human heritage. This in turn may help him to both criticize and appreciate his own inheritance. He can read and study. For the young man who is determined to make the most of his time in service tremendous opportunities are there for the taking.

But Hazards Are There, Too . . .

A religious word for the non-combatant hazards of military life is "temptation." Whether civilian or serviceman, the young adult becomes free to indulge himself in women, drink, foul language and general coarseness, smoking, and, more recently, narcotics. In military service the debasing possibilities seem grosser, more immediate and vivid than in civilian life. They assault a man more boldly. In his uniform the GI is a marked man; in every town there will be people waiting to victimize him. His very inexperience makes him vulnerable. Mistakenly, he may identify indulgences with manliness. The normal restraints of family and home are withdrawn.

Every man brings his strengths and weaknesses with him into service. He is what he is—as well as what he is becoming. The pressure to "go with the crowd," to carouse, and yield to one's lowest instincts will be strong. Yet, it is not different elsewhere in life. No man *has* to accept the worst kind of companions. On his off-duty time a serviceman can go as high or as low as he wishes. He makes or breaks himself. The Services offer libraries, craft shops, education programs, sports of all types, tours at bargain rates, free tickets to good shows, chapel activities, civilian invitations, and a host of other attractions. All the Services encourage a man to be his best self. The recruit should "take it easy" until he learns the rules of the road.

"The Woes of the Soldier" [1]

It has been the thesis of this chapter that life offers essentially the same experiences to all men and that the context of an experience merely alters its intensity. When military forces are needed no longer, a chapter in man's ancient experience with misery and suffering will end. A new day will be at hand. Until that day, we shall need soldiers. Like other men, they will face hardship. The Armed Forces are proficient at getting men into top physical condition; the imposition of hardship is an indispensable part of the process. The instruction is neither pleasant nor useless. It is preparation for what lies ahead. The exhaustion from hours spent out-of-doors, from night-time operations that permit no sleep, from the cruelest and extremest of discomforts in all climates is something no man would choose for himself, much less impose upon others. Yet, what conquest in any realm is easy? In the mysterious providence of God, hardship, pain, and suffering have a place in the making of a man.

Fear and Combat

Though probably not more than three soldiers in ten engage in combat in war-time, all must prepare for it. In basic training the recruit may have his first encounter with fear. Live ammunition is used. He learns to hug the "good" earth. He acquires a healthy respect for the things that can hurt him. No man goes knowingly under hostile fire without a sense of apprehension. His well-being virtually requires it. His survival is at stake. Yet, he soon discovers that survival and fear are in opposition, that the will to survive is stronger. In combat a man is often too busy to dwell on fear. In the crucial moments his training shows itself and, almost automatically, he does what is necessary. Fear as a paralyzing force is behind him. He has passed through.

---

[1] The theme of a vivid passage on the life of a soldier in ancient Egypt, in *Never to Die: The Egyptians in Their Own Words,* by Josephine Mayer and Tom Prideaux, Viking Press, 1958; also quoted in H. Felsen, *To My Son in Uniform,* N.Y. Dodd, Mead, 1966, pp. 20-21. A few expressions from "the Woes": "His masters are many . . . he is driven about like a donkey . . . He is hungry, his body is worn out, he is dead while yet alive . . . He marchest high up in the mountains . . . The foe lieth hidden in the scrub . . . They say to him, 'Forward brave soldier, win for thyself a good name.' But he is half-conscious, his knees are loosed, and his head paineth him . . ."

BIBLIOGRAPHY

Fiction

Nearly 100 titles are listed under "Soldier" in the *Fiction Catalogue*, 7th ed. 1960, H. W. Wilson & Co., N.Y., pp. 612-13. Twelve nations, including ancient Rome, are represented. Among the titles are:

Three Soldiers by J. Dos Passos
The Red Badge of Courage by S. Crane
Men at War by Ernest Hemingway, the best war stories of all times. Berkley, 4th printing, 1968. 505 pp. $1.25.
From Here to Eternity by J. Jones
Memoirs of an Infantry Officer by S. Sassoon
The Naked and the Dead by N. Mailer
All Quiet on the Western Front by E. M. Remarque
And Quiet Flows the Don by M. Sholokhov
War and Peace by L. Tolstoy

Non-Fiction

Letters from Vietnam edited by Bill Adler, N.Y. E. P. Dutton & Co., 1967, 212 pp., $3.95.
The Letters of Pfc. Richard E. Marks, USMC, N.Y. J. B. Lippincott Co., 1967, pp. 190, $3.95.
Postmark: Mekong Delta by Raymond W. Johnson, N.Y. Fleming H. Revell Co., 1968, pp. 96, $2.95.
The New Legions by Donald Duncan, N.Y. Random House, 1967, pp. 275.
This Damn Tree Leaks by William H. Mauldin, N.Y. Simon & Shuster, 1945, pp. 117.
Up Front by William H. Mauldin, N.Y. H. Holt & Co., 1945, pp. 228.
Bill Mauldin's Army, N.Y., W. Sloan Ass., 1951, pp. 383.
Bill Mauldin in Korea, N.Y., W. W. Norton, 1952, pp. 171.
Soldier Life in the Union and Confederate Armies by Philip Van Doren Stern, Bloomington, Ind. Press, 1961, pp. 400.
Hardtack & Coffee by John Davis Billings, the unwritten story of army life, Chicago, Lakeside Press, 1960, pp. 483.
The British Soldier by Col. H. De Watteville, N.Y. G. P. Putnam & Sons, 1954, pp. 242.

Chapter 12

The Serviceman Overseas

THERE is great likelihood that the average draftee or enlistee will draw at least one tour of duty outside of continental United States. In mid-1967 one third of our active forces were stationed overseas in an estimated eighty-two countries.[1] Servicemen are attached to nearly all U.S. consulates. A breakdown of the overseas deployment of American servicemen as of June 30, 1967 looked like this:*

Atlantic Area		Pacific Area	
Canada	3,000	Thailand	43,000
Bermuda	2,000	So. Vietnam	522,000
England	25,000	Navy	35,000
Greenland	1,500	Philippines	30,000
Iceland	3,000	Guam	10,000
Spain	10,000	Taiwan (Classified)	
Latin America	40,000	Okinawa	40,000
West Germany	257,000	South Korea	55,000
Middle-East, Africa	10,000	Japan	40,000

In both the Atlantic and Pacific areas many GIs have their families with them. In December, 1963 about 155,000 children attended 291 service-operated schools in 28 countries. They were taught by 6,000 civilian teachers. When to these service-connected individuals one adds an estimated two million American civilians who work and reside overseas, the reality of a very large Yankee diaspora becomes clear.

Opportunity and Responsibility

Travel abroad is both an opportunity and a responsibility. It is an opportunity to discover how the rest of the world lives, thinks, believes, and feels. Its educational value is considerable and has not been over-estimated. It offers lessons unavailable in classrooms.

* Associated Press Newsfeatures, 4/2/68

But travel also means responsibility. Overseas the traveler incarnates his country. Strangers form their impressions of a distant place from its living representatives. How important for the world is this when the travelers are Americans!

The role, therefore, of American troops overseas in such large numbers is critically important to the shaping of the world's image of the U.S. This is fully realized by our government. Its Defense and State Departments have developed innumerable programs, films, guides, and courses to prepare our troops for what they will encounter on overseas tours. There is no need for a GI to go uninformed. He will receive orientation lectures both before and after arrival at an overseas post. He can take courses in the local languages at no cost. His country is eager that he be its best possible representative and it expects him to work at it. Most of the time he has been precisely this. He has won much affection and respect. A reputation for generosity and love of children precedes him wherever he goes. The job of ambassador is not easy—particularly for soldiers. There is bound to be resentment and tension between a local population and the troops of a foreign government who are on the scene, whatever the reason for their presence. In the light of this consideration, the performance of American GIs has been remarkable. They have won their way despite the barriers created by their association with affluence and power.

The serviceman who is also a Christian will have a special obligation to see others as Christ sees them, to make every effort to understand them, and to treat them as Christ would do. But he should be warned that he may be in for a period of "cultural shock." Not only may he find himself unwelcome at first, but, though he may begin with the best intentions, he may find it hard to love people who have strange customs. Patience, restraint, a demeanor of unfailing courtesy, and steady persistence are called for. He will have to earn his acceptance as a person, as a Christian, and as an American. If he succeeds, his country need have no fears.

Some Suggestions

In a helpful new pamphlet, the United Presbyterian Church offers these suggestions to servicemen who are heading overseas:[2]

- Establish high moral standards for your own conduct.
- Accept people as they are.
- When you speak with others, or about others, do so with respect.

- Do not compare the United States to your advantage with everybody you meet.
- Learn to say "please" and "thank you" in the language of the people.
- Learn the language as rapidly as you can.
- Use your knowledge and goods to help people in trouble without being patronizing.
- Offer your services to the chaplains of your unit.
- Meet with others for study, discussion and prayer.
- Remain intellectually curious and adventurous about the culture of the country where you are serving.
- Use your imagination and ingenuity and develop the resources of your Christian faith.

The Serviceman and Overseas Churches

Chaplains may be able to assist servicemen in establishing contact with civilian congregations overseas. Additionally, the Overseas Missions Departments at denominational headquarters can provide names and addresses of personnel in overseas churches. The GIs home clergyman can give him a letter of introduction which will help to open doors.

Enduring personal ties of friendship and shared faith can result from seeking out an indigenous congregation on a foreign shore and from making the effort to identify with it.

The Military Family Overseas

A serviceman alerted to go overseas will know whether or not his family can accompany him. Dependents of privates and seamen may not thus travel abroad. If a man is permitted to bring his wife and children, the government will generally assist him with their travel and will move his furniture. Medical coverage is provided, and the family may shop at the PX and Commissary. A number of books and other publications are available to guide wives who face the twin problems of moving a household overseas and of replanting it among people with strange languages and stranger customs.

The government also operates free schools for the minor children of servicemen and civilians serving it overseas.* These are staffed by

*For a listing of these schools cf. *Uniformed Services Almanac*, 1968 edition, pp. 54-6. Address: P.O. Box 400, Washington, D.C. 20004; $1.25, 152 pp.

well-qualified teachers and administrators from public school systems in the U.S. In some areas children attend private schools. Tuition is paid by the service. Where schools are not available correspondence courses are provided without charge to the family.

It must be remarked once more that the benefits of the overseas experience will be in proportion to the family's ability to adapt itself sympathetically to a foreign and sometimes even hostile culture.

Hospitality Centers

Through its Committee on Ministry to Service Personnel in the Far East, the National Council of Churches of Christ in the U.S.A. operates hospitality centers in Japan, Korea, Okinawa, Hong Kong, and Thailand.**

Additionally, the Lutheran Council of the United States of America maintains centers in Germany, Guam, Japan, Korea, Okinawa, the Philippines, and Thailand.***

The Seventh-Day Adventist also operate several centers. For information write Seventh-Day Adventist Church, National Service Organization, 6840 Eastern Ave., N.W., Washington, D.C. 20012.

The United Service Organizations (USO)

USO is the cooperative program of six Member Agencies; Young Men's Christian Associations, National Catholic Community Service, National Jewish Welfare Board, Young Women's Christian Association, The Salvation Army and Traveler's Aid Association of America. USO Shows, representing the finest of America's musical and variety talent, entertain military personnel in all parts of the world. USO clubs operate overseas under the direct cognizance of the Department of Defense and offer the traditional "home away from home atmosphere" complete with snack bars, libraries, recording devices, overseas telephone services, checking facilities, and religious referrals.

At the end of 1967 the USO provided its programs and services for American GIs in thirty-seven places overseas, excluding Vietnam. In Vietnam it had seventeen centers with a professional staff of forty-

**For a listing of addresses and the Committee's semi-annual *News,* describing activities at these centers write to the Committee at 475 Riverside Drive, Room 665, New York, N.Y.   10027.
***Full information about these is available from the Division of Service to Military Personnel, 2633 16th St. N.W., Washington, D.C.   20009.

seven. Attendance at these was averaging 650,000 per month. The military audience for USO shows around the world hit 6.2 million, up three million from 1966. In the U.S. the USO operated programs in 121 communities. 1,834 Community Chests and United Funds included the USO in their allocation budgets. (Clergymen can urge that the USO be included in fair-share budgets of local funds.) 113,000 volunteers worked for the USO in 1967. The organization also works to interest churches and synagogues in ministering to service personnel. Its national headquarters is at 237 E. 52nd St. New York, N.Y. 10022 (Phone, 212-751-3020). It publishes a monthly bulletin, USO NEWS.

Encountering Unfamiliar Religions

Perhaps the most demanding of the encounters experienced by Americans overseas are those with persons professing unfamiliar religions and practicing totally unfamiliar religious customs. This is a particularly important consideration in the Far East, the Near and Middle East, and Africa. For American servicemen these encounters began in earnest during the Allied sweep across the Pacific during World War II. They were a crucial factor in the "successful" occupation of Japan and were met once more during the Korean War. Now, in Vietnam and all through Southeast Asia, young Americans in great numbers are living, working, and dying among Buddhists, Taoists, Shintoists, and Hindus.

The government tries to brief servicemen on the religious scruples and traditions of Asian peoples. It publishes leaflets and pamphlets. In addition, the Judeo-Christian churches of the West are paying more and more attention to the beliefs of Easterners. The Vatican maintains an office for liaison with Non-Christian religions. Much good material is in print, and numerous courses are available. A sampling of books and other items is offered in the bibliography at the end of this chapter. Clergymen should urge their young adults to read up on the religions of the countries to which they may be assigned. Parish libraries could well devote a shelf to this topic—one of fundamental importance to future relationships between East and West.

Humanitarian Projects Overseas

American servicemen have demonstrated concern and ingenuity in supporting relief and rehabilitation programs all over the world. In spare time and without other sponsorship they have undertaken innumerable projects and have summoned assistance from citizens and companies back home. Many GIs are interested in the overseas relief programs of their denominations. Their gifts to one agency alone (Church World Service) total $50,000-$60,000 per year. They obtain information about these programs in advance by directing inquiries either to the Christian Social Service agency at their denominational headquarters, or by writing:

CHURCH WORLD SERVICE
475 Riverside Drive
New York, N.Y.   10027

or

CATHOLIC RELIEF SERVICES
U.S.C.C.
350 Fifth Avenue, N.Y., N.Y.   10001

NOTES

1. Source: *Uniformed Services Almanac,* 1968 edition, p. 151. Total outside the U.S.—1,128,129, not including 450,040 afloat & mobile.
2. *Christian Servicemen Abroad,* leaflet published by the Commission on Ecumenical Missions and Relations, Room 922, 475 Riverside Drive, New York, N.Y.   10027, quoted by permission. Has a booklist.

BIBLIOGRAPHY

There are many excellent publications on various aspects of the American presence abroad. Some of those most pertinent to the Armed Forces context are given here.

Books

Your Assignment Overseas by Vernon Pizer and Perry H. Davis, II, a Handbook for the Serviceman and His Family, 1st edition, New York, W. W. Norton Co., 1955, 291 pp. Describes duty and living conditions in 24 countries.

The Navy Wife by Nancy B. Shea and Anne E. Pye, 4th revised edition, N.Y. Harper, 1966. Interprets military life primarily, but not exclusively, as it is known by officers' wives. Has a chapter on family life overseas.

Sailor's Wife by Lucy G. Wright, U.S. Naval Institute, 1962. By a seaman's wife.

The Army Wife by Nancy B. Shea, 3rd revised edition, N.Y. Harper 1954, 637 pp. Has a chapter on army life overseas from a wife's point of view.

Leaflets

Can Your Faith Travel? "Training Suggestions for Overseasmanship", Published by Committee on American Laymen Overseas, National Council of Churches, 475 Riverside Drive, New York, N.Y. 10027. Very helpful for its reading lists.

Overseas American Series—World Horizons, Room 1268 A, 475 Riverside Drive, New York, N.Y. 10027

American Laymen Abroad
Christians in Government Abroad
Laymen and Christian Churches Abroad
Christians in American Communities Abroad

A Guide to English Language Congregations in Selected Cities Overseas. Pub'd by the Churchmen Overseas Program, National Council of Churches, 475 Riverside Drive, New York, N.Y. 10027.

Going Abroad? "See the Relief and Rehabilitation Ministries of Your Church in Action" Describes projects of Church World Service, National Council of Churches, 475 Riverside Drive, New York, N.Y. 10027, and gives names and addresses of contact persons for each.

Newspaper

Pacific STARS AND STRIPES, especially its Orientation Editions, viz, Summer-Fall, 1967, published by the Office of Information, Military Assistance Command, Vietnam (MACV), APO San Francisco, Calif. 96222.

Chapter 13

Marriage and Military Service

THERE are large numbers of married men in all branches of the
Armed Forces. Just how many is uncertain, for the high transiency among military personnel and their movement into and out of
the service makes the gathering of statistics very difficult. Neither the
Defense Department nor the Bureau of the Census can offer much
current information. However, over 188,000 children of servicemen
attend government-operated schools in the U.S. and overseas, and
additional thousands are in public schools of the U.S. (Many of these
latter schools, being close to military installations, receive special
grants from the Department of Defense.) A source in the Army Information office in New York City estimates that the average number of
dependents per married man in the Armed Forces is 2.3 (Spring,
1968). On this basis the children attending government-operated
schools alone represent 144,615 families.

Housing is another indicator. The Defense Department's family
housing appropriation request for Fiscal Year 1969 is $589 million
dollars, of which $48.7 million is for construction of new units (against
$155 million in '68) and the rest for operation and maintenance of an
inventory of 363,792 housing units. Thousands of other families find
their own housing off the post.

There is a constant traffic of wives, children, and household goods
as men move from assignment to assignment around the world. At
any given moment dozens of military air terminals are crowded with
dependents on the move.

Married personnel tend to be careerists, although married men are
now being drafted. In the enlisted ranks the married men are usually
in the upper grades—E-4 and above—chiefly because pay scales be-
neath these grades will not support a family. Nevertheless, there are
many married privates. In their struggle to keep the family together
they "moonlight" in the civilian economy, and their wives work. The
enlistee or draftee (pay grade E-1) receives $102.30 per month. His

94

maximum pay for the first two years will be $137.50 per month (E-3, Pfc). Allowances for housing and dependents are inadequate. The going is rough.

In 1966 in the U.S. there were an estimated 1,844,000 marriages—an average of 5,052 per day. Many of these involved young men standing on the threshold of military service. It has been suggested that conscription has tended to accelerate a trend toward early marriage.[1]

Reasons for this include

- the hope of escaping military service by becoming fathers,
- the sense of urgency created by prospect of his being removed from the presence of the young woman he is courting,
- the first steady pay, despite its inadequacy,
- a fear of loneliness and of being catapulted into the unknown without a familiar companion.

Military service is but one of the factors fostering earlier marriages. Together, the result is that about one quarter of all young women marry before they reach eighteen, and over one-half are married before they reach twenty-one. One male college student in four is married. For every 100 girls of ages 18-22 there are only 91 boys of ages 20-24. Today a young man does not have to choose between a career and a wife—very often he can have both.

The Role of the Chaplain

Since his "parishioners" are in precisely the age bracket in which most American males commit themselves to that venerable institution known as "holy matrimony," the military chaplain expends a large proportion of his work week on some aspect or other of marriage. He devotes much more time to this than do his civilian colleagues. If he is a career chaplain, it is possible that the services have sent him to graduate school for training as a marriage counselor. He talks with young servicemen and their fiancees, and he officiates at their weddings in the installation chapel. What civilian cleric can match the experience of the chaplains at one of the Service academies who during a single week in June may officiate at the marriage of one-third to one-half of the graduating class—200 to 400 weddings, one every half-hour for days?

On every installation the chaplain spends much time listening to couples air their problems.

He ministers to military families much as do civilian clergymen.

Often these are "waiting" families, the men being away. Always there is danger lurking in the background. More frequently than is the case with civilian clergymen, the chaplain is called upon to tell a waiting wife that she is a widow.

His Ecclesiastical Status

With respect to marriage the chaplain is at one with civilian clergymen, except that he may have a heavier concentration of work in this area. Legally (and usually canonically) he is no different from them and functions as they do by virtue of ordination. He is not bound by military regulations respecting his ecclesiastical prerogatives. At his discretion or by the canons of his denomination he may decline to officiate at any proposed marriage. With regard to mixed marriages the chaplain will reflect the attitudes—and the canons—of his denomination. This will be true also with respect to the remarriage of divorced persons.

Like civilian clergymen, he must ascertain that the laws of the State or territory within which a marriage occurs are complied with. In many States he himself must obtain special license or bonding as an out-of-state clergyman. The couple must obtain a civil license even though their marriage occurs on Federal "territory." The chaplain makes the normal return to civil authority and reports his official acts to his Chief of Chaplains and to his denominational superior.

Overseas Marriages

Servicemen who marry overseas must comply with local statutes, and an enlisted man normally must obtain the permission of his commanding officer. The U.S. Government has consular agreements concerning marriage of its troops with nationals of the countries in which Americans are stationed. Details about this—and about the admission of a foreign-born spouse to the United States—may be had at American consulates abroad. Many countries do not accord legal status to religious marriages and require that a separate civil ceremony occur *before* the church wedding. All American citizens contemplating marriage in foreign lands should consult the nearest American consulate.

Military Marriages Involving Civilian Clergymen

A civilian clergyman cannot officiate at any religious service on a military installation except by invitation of its senior chaplain or commanding officer. This includes marriages. If a couple desires a clergyman's participation they should request the chaplain to extend him an invitation. He and the civilian cleric will work out arrangements together, it being understood that the chaplain is in charge—as the civilian clergyman would be were the marriage occurring in his church with the chaplain assisting.

Now and again chaplain and civilian clergy will have to "team up" to deal with the thicket of civil, military, ecclesiastical, and pastoral difficulties which marital problems of service personnel can present. The civilian should be prepared to hold up his end. Often the chaplain may be an unknown, distant figure, and misunderstandings may arise. The civilian clergyman should realize that certain military ground rules will apply. A chaplain may need background material or other information from a serviceman's home community. He may write or telephone the man's pastor. Clergy near military installations can sometimes materially assist their military colleagues.

Family Life in the Armed Forces

As certain families have for decades—and even for centuries—been identified with law, medicine, politics, or the church, others have produced generations of soldiers. Such is still the case in many instances, although the tradition becomes steadily more difficult to maintain and transmit. The military family is subject to many more strains today. While on the one hand it struggles to cling to old patterns, it is responding simultaneously to developments which tend to give it more of the characteristics of civilian family life. Though far from complete and doubtless not destined to become so, the transition has progressed far enough to receive close daily attention both within and outside the military establishment. The career military officer, anciently epitemized as "an officer and a gentleman," must now combine the old professional standards and images with the new necessity that he be a competent manager and administrator—the military counterpart of countless civilian executives.

The nature of the military calling has changed so sharply that many fine officers are led to question their continuance in it. They judge themselves increasingly by civilian as well as by military standards and at times find the comparison damaging. They confront real tension between the demands of their profession and those of their families. As often as not the decision is for family; attrition rates are high. Family relations do not conform as closely to professional requirements as they once did.

It is impossible to extend the space allotted to this sizeable and significant subject. A growing literature about it is on hand.[2] It should be pointed out in summation that the technological developments of World War II and of the post-War period have revolutionized life on this planet. The American military establishment, far from being exempt from change, is still in the throes of adjustment. This is reflected in the placing of new strains upon relationships in military families. Such also, however, is the lot of civilian families today. Things are not as they were—for anybody.

It should be noted that the various hospitality centers, both in the U.S. and overseas, also minister to military families. USO has "waiting Wives Clubs" and several family service programs. It publishes a wide range of pastoral literature. For details, write to USO National Headquarters (cf. pp. 90-91).

NOTES AND BIBLIOGRAPHY

1. *The Optimistic Tradition of American Youth* by Eli Ginzberg, *op cit.*, pp. 86-92, a very helpful discussion of military service as a factor contributing to early marriage.

2. For a penetrating and illuminating discussion of family life for professional military officers see *The Professional Soldier* by Morris Janowitz, esp. Chapter 9, pp. 175 ff. and "Family Relations," pp. 187-195. Free Press Paperback, 1964.

For discussions of U.S. marriage statistics, see:

This U.S.A.: An Unexpected Family Portrait of 197,926,341 Americans Drawn from the Census, by Ben J. Wattenberg, Pocket Books, N.Y., 1967, pp. 40-52.
200 Million Americans by Clarence M. Wright, Bureau of the Census, Nov. 1967, pp. 19-23; Government Printing Office, Washington, D.C. 20402; $1.00.

On Marriage Counseling:

Premarital Counseling: A Manual for Ministers, A Psychologically and Theologically Oriented Guide to Christian Marriage, by J. Kenneth Morris, Prentice-Hall, Inc., Englewood Cliffs, N.J. 1960, 229 pp.

On Marriage and Military Service (for young couples)

Before You Marry in the Service, booklet by Captain Frederick W. Brink, CHC, USN, Revised, 1964 & 1966, published by the Department of Chaplains and Service Personnel, United Presbyterian Church, USA, 4125 Nebraska Ave., N.W. Wash., D.C. 20016, 28 pp.

Called to Serve, including a chapter on Preparing for a Successful Marriage (pp. 52-64), by Commander David W. Plank, CHC, USN. Offers Christian counsel to servicemen contemplating marriage, plus some suggestions for married servicemen on dealing with separation in military family life. Published by the Gospel Publishing House, Springfield, Mo. 65802, 1967. This is a general book on military service by an Assembly of God clergyman. $1.95.

Sex, Love, Marriage, and the Home, a booklet, reprint from LINK Magazine, containing seven essays on aspects of marriage. Has a most helpful, 2-page bibliography; Published by the General Commission on Chaplains and Armed Forces Personnel, 122 Maryland Avenue, N.E., Washington, D.C. 20002. 20¢, 29 pp.

The Catholic Family in Uniform by the Rev. E. Schmiedeler and Chaplain, Col. Constantine E. Zielinski, USAF, 10th Printing, 1966, National Catholic Community Service, 1312 Massachusetts Ave., Washington, D.C. 20005, 37 pp. For Service Personnel.

The Serviceman and Marriage, No. 4 in Series of Six entitled *Serving a Great Country* by the Rev. Edward V. Stanford, O.S.A. National Catholic Community Service, 9th printing, April, 1966.

cf. also publications of the Family Life Bureau, U.S. Catholic Conference, 1312 Massachusetts Ave., N.W., Washington, D.C. 20005.

Chapter 14

Emergencies Involving Servicemen

IN meeting emergency situations military chaplains and civilian clergymen have a common pastoral concern and responsibility. Here above all, the ministry is one. Every crisis involving a serviceman has civilian ramifications; many crises involving civilians affect servicemen. A soldier's morale is acutely sensitive to the well-being of his family.

The chaplain's first pastoral responsibility is the man in uniform. Dependents come next. They may be accessible to civilian clergymen; normally, this will depend on the military housing pattern, the preferences of the family, and command policies. Civilian clerics should learn and use the proper channels whenever they work among military personnel. On a base they should obtain clearance from the senior chaplain or the commander. This is of great importance.

Crises Within Military Life: Legal

"I, . . . , do solemnly swear that I will bear true faith and allegiance to the United States of America; that I will serve them honestly and faithfully against all their enemies whomsoever; and that I will obey the President of the United States and the orders of the officers appointed over me, according to the regulations and the Uniform Code of Military Justice. So help me God!"

The young person who affirms this oath at the Armed Forces induction Center becomes subject to military law. Passed by Congress on May 31, 1951, the "Uniform Code" sets forth the serviceman's rights, the offenses for which he may be tried, and the punishments which may be imposed. It is generally consistent with civilian statutes[1]— to which he also remains subject. Certain of the Code's 140 Articles are read to recruits as part of the swearing-in procedure. Cruel and unusual punishments, including flogging, are prohibited. In military life the innocent are rarely convicted, and the guilty are rarely acquitted.

Lesser offenses, not truly "crimes," usually draw punishment meted out by the commanding officer. In order of their seriousness, graver offenses are handled by courts-martial—Summary, Special, and General. As its name implies, the Summary Court is prompt, swiftly concluded, and normally entrusted to one officer. It tries enlisted men only. The Special Court-Martial is the intermediate court and usually consists of two officers and an enlisted man. It can impose a bad conduct discharge. The General Court-Martial is reserved for cases of the utmost gravity and may decree a wide range of penalties, including death. All court-martial cases are subject to at least two appellate reviews and in some circumstances three. Chaplains may testify at courts-martial, but may not serve as a court member.

The Judge Advocate

Every large military unit has a legal officer, called the judge advocate. His job is to provide legal advice to the commander and to military personnel. He prepares legal documents and administers oaths. He participates in courts-martial and upon request of an accused serviceman may be assigned as defense counsel. He cannot represent a serviceman before a civilian court. The following points should be kept in mind:

1. A serviceman has the right of privileged communication. The legal officer cannot be ordered to divulge information given in confidence and will not do so without express permission.
2. The views of the judge advocate do not bind either the Armed Forces or the Government. In some situations, however, he does legally represent the Government.
3. Servicemen should not sign contracts without first consulting the legal officer. They should bring all pertinent data.
4. The wife, parents, or clergyman of a serviceman facing a court-martial should consult the legal officer for information and for suggestions as to the most helpful courses of action.
5. Absence without leave is a serious offense (cf. Art. 86 of the Code). Everything should be done to dissuade a serviceman from going AWOL. Dependents and friends of an AWOL GI should bend every effort to persuade him to return—quickly.

Discharges

An honorable discharge from military service is valuable. A dishonorable discharge can cause (1) loss of almost all Federal and State veteran's benefits; (2) loss of citizenship and voting rights; (3) ineligibility for employment opportunity; (4) disqualification for financial bonding; (5) loss of standing in the community and ineligibility for public office. The main types of discharges are: Honorable, General, Undesirable, Bad Conduct, and Dishonorable. It is important that discharge records be accurate. Each service has a board for the correction of military records. The Veterans Administration can supply information about this.

Crisis Within Military Life: Medical

When serious illness or injury hospitalizes a serviceman, his next-of-kin is notified promptly, usually by telegram. On a military installation his family can get information through the Personal Affairs office. The chaplain can help. Otherwise, the nearest chapter of the American Red Cross is the best source of assistance. Through its national headquarters in Washington each local chapter can communicate with the Red Cross field worker attached to every military hospital. In the U.S. military hospitals are located on large installations. They often can accommodate visitors for short stays. Chaplains are stationed at military hospitals.

Wounded in Action

When a man is wounded in action, first aid is administered by combat medical personnel until it is possible to remove him to a field hospital. The helicopter has greatly reduced the time lapse between injury and hospitalization—with consequent improvement of medical prognosis. The man usually remains at the field hospital for a very short time; as quickly as his injuries permit, he is sent to a rear area hospital for further treatment and evaluation. Next-of-kin are notified promptly by wire. Each service has casualty notification units on duty around the clock. Their personnel are trained and equipped to offer anxious families every possible assistance. Inquiries can also be sent via the Red Cross. Next-of-kin can write or wire the man's commanding officer.

If prolonged hospitalization is indicated, the man is flown back to the U.S. in specially equipped Med-Evac planes. Details about each Med-Evac flight are released forty-eight hours in advance. Movement depends, of course, upon the man's condition and upon flying conditions. Casualty assistance offices can provide flight information. Patients are normally sent to the military hospital equipped to handle their case nearest their home.

Men who recover fully are returned to duty. Those with only slight disability are retained and assigned to duties within their capability. In cases of serious disability medical discharges are granted upon recommendation of special medical boards. The boards, working in conjunction with the Veterans Administration, also determine eligibility for disability pensions. Sometimes the true extent of a man's disability does not become evident for a year or more.

Killed, Missing in Action, or Captured

When a serviceman is confirmed as killed or missing in action the report is radioed to Washington and goes from there to the service headquarters nearest the man's home. An officer is dispatched to break the news personally. He will often stop at a church in the neighborhood. Clergymen are of great help to these Notification Officers in this saddest and most difficult of assignments.

The officer stays with the family as long as he feels he can be useful. After his visit the service sends a confirming telegram and, later, a second, asking instructions regarding delivery of the body. This usually arrives in seven to ten days. It is escorted by a member of the Armed Forces. The deceased's commanding officer will usually write to the family.

A second officer is assigned to assist the family with burial arrangements, financial and other matters. Since these involve the Veterans Administration, he is familiar with its policies. For the distraught family, therefore, he provides liaison with both the military and the agency to which it now must turn.

Procedure is much the same for men reported missing in action. Next-of-kin receive all confirmed information promptly. Every effort is made to account for each man.

Word of a man's capture is relayed by telegram. Servicemen are taught how to behave if captured and learn the major provisions of the Geneva Convention. Their captors may or may not honor them. The most experienced resource is the International Red Cross. Families should request its assistance via the national headquarters of the American Red Cross, Washington, D.C. 20006. All available information about the capture should be supplied.

Crises at Home

Should trouble arise at home, servicemen want to know about it—fast. Through the Red Cross it is very simple to get word quickly to a serviceman overseas. Before a commander will release a man for a long, costly trip home, he requires authentication of the need. This is where the Red Cross comes in. Its charter "imposes . . . the duties to act as the medium of voluntary relief and communication between the American people and their Armed Forces." It can get action rapidly. This is its job. It handles over 700 emergency messages a day to and from Vietnam alone.

The family or its representative should go to the nearest Red Cross chapter and outline the situation to its Service to Military Families worker. It should bring full documentation, i.e. letters or other attestation from clergymen and attending physicians. The local chapter will telephone or wire the Red Cross Emergency Center in Washington. A message will go to its Field Director assigned to the man's unit. He or the chaplain will convey the news. Decision as to the man's release rests with the commander. A man on emergency leave flies via military aircraft to the nearest U.S. coast. He may have to use commercial flights to his home. The Red Cross makes loans or grants for travel and living expense.

Through his unit's Field Director a serviceman overseas can obtain information about crises at home. He can also request the local Red Cross chapter to assist his distant family. Red Cross assistance is *not* available for the following: repayment or consolidation of debts; business ventures; marital conflict and divorce; pregnancy out of wedlock; posting of bail, employment of counsel, and payment of fines; and implementation of service pay to cover unreasonable expenditures.

"Compassionate" Reassignment; Hardship Discharges

A continuing crisis at home may require a man's presence for a longer period. A "compassionate transfer" may be indicated. In support of such a petition the serviceman must present letters from a clergyman and/or doctor and two other persons, not relatives. The commanding officer may seek a confidential report on the home situation via the Red Cross. The Navy grants such transfers for not more than six months. In an application for compassionate discharge it is necessary to show how the action proposed will solve the problem. Documentation should be notarized or put on letterhead stationery.

Miscellaneous Crises at Home

"His girl has discovered that she's going to have a baby. Can he be ordered back to marry her?" No, nor will he get emergency leave. If regular leave is due him, it will be routinely granted. The services do not initiate investigations in such cases. The chaplain and possibly the legal officer should be consulted.

"His wife isn't getting any money." She should write her husband's commanding officer. If the failure is deliberate the CO can order him to make out an allotment in her favor.

"He hasn't written in months. Is he all right?" Men are sometimes unable to send letters. Polaris submariners on patrol can't. Upon request, however, the local Red Cross chapter will make inquiry. Usually, a letter follows forthwith.

Military Welfare Organizations

"The Red Cross and the military welfare agencies (Navy Relief Society, Army Emergency Relief, and Air Force Aid Society) have agreed on policies and procedures to facilitate mutual cooperation in providing financial assistance to service personnel and their dependents. Although their financial assistance policies appear to be nearly parallel, there are situations in which the Red Cross and the military agency can assist and other situations in which one cannot assist and the other can. Appropriate referrals . . . are made." The USO is also very helpful in emergencies. It maintains lounges at some airports; the Traveler's Aid Association of America is a USO agency. Many USO units offer "locator service" and assist in emergency housing. The chaplain will know about the resources of the respective agencies.

NOTES AND BIBLIOGRAPHY

1. Though it represented a vast improvement over the military law of World War II, the Code is now considered to lag behind contemporary legal standards. Interest in overhauling it is growing. The American Veterans Committee sponsored a national conference on the Human Rights of the Man in the Uniform in 1968 in Washington, D.C.

The Serviceman and the Law by Col. M. O. Edwards and Col. C. L Diecker, Harrisburg, Pa., the Military Service Publishing Co., 3rd printing, 6th Edition, 1955, 403 pp. A real compendium on this subject.

Every Serviceman's Lawyer by Earl Synder, Harrisburg, Pa., The Stackpole Co., 1960, 341 pp. More popularly written and extremely helpful.

Red Cross Services for the United States Armed Forces, Red Cross pamphlet No. 2015, July, 1963, 17 pp. A spelling out of Red Cross assistance programs.

Chapter 15

When He Becomes a Civilian Again

O VER twenty-six million American men and women are veterans of military service. Twenty-two million have served in war-time. The impact of this upon American society has been incalculable.

How can you . . . estimate the national homogeneity achieved by the barracks mix of rich and poor, city slicker and rural rube, rural slicker and city rube, of the educated and the uneducated, the literate and the semi-literate and more recently, of white and Negro? What . . . rubs off on whom and what doesn't? . . . Military experience is a truly enormous common national tie . . . [1]

The 1960 Census—the first to publish detailed figures on veterans —reveals that

• Veterans are much better educated than non-veterans (12.1 years of school vs. 9.4 years of school).

• Veterans are more mobile than non-veterans (52% moved from 1955 to 1960 vs. 43% for non-vets).

• Veterans earn more money than non-veterans ($5109 per year for veterans vs. $3215 for non-veterans).

• The average veteran is younger than the average non-veteran (thirty-eight vs. forty-five years).

• Veterans are disproportionately likely to be white (of males over fourteen years of age about 28% of the non-whites have seen military service, compared with 39% of the whites).

• Veterans are more urban than rural. (Of all urban males over fourteen, 42% were veterans. For rural males, the veteran rate is just 22%.) [2]

Whatever discounting of the above figures may be possible, "the

106

basic sociological correlation holds: veterans are wealthier, better educated, more mobile, etc., than are non-veterans.[2] Military service has opened doorways to self-improvement and has given millions a "common national tie." Reckoned beside the fearful cost of war, this is a small benefit. Yet a benefit it clearly is.

The Returning Serviceman in 1968

750,000 veterans re-enter civilian life each year. Over 300,000 Vietnam veterans ("Vietvets") are now civilians. This includes 41,000 Negroes. Many "Vietvets" are twenty-two or twenty-three. Others are careerists, with twenty to thirty years of active duty. Not all have been in Vietnam.

What are they like? How do they differ from veterans of World War II and the Korean War? Has society changed during their absence? How can it assist them as they return? What can church people do?

They're All Different

If one asks, "What will the returning serviceman be like?," the reply given in 1945 by J. Gordon Chamberlin still holds:

There cannot be any single type. The millions of different individuals who form the armed forces of America have gone through millions of wartime experiences. Some generalities may be true of men of certain ranks, of certain theaters of combat, of certain branches of the service, of particular denominations, age, marital status, educational background, prewar occupation, moral record, type of wound, or mental condition. But even these are subject to constant change.[3]

There is one striking difference. Whereas in 1945 America had to brace itself for the mass return of 7,000,000 overseas veterans, the men come back today almost one-by-one. They slip back into their communities literally overnight and in almost total anonymity. The community scarcely knew that they had gone—let alone that they survived and have come back. As they drop out of sight it becomes difficult to keep track of them. The Vietvets have not yet surfaced as a group.[4]

Today's veterans return swiftly. From combat patrol in Vietnam, from Germany, Ethiopia, Japan, Greenland, and Antarctica they get home in twelve to forty-eight hours. The abruptness of the change may be traumatic. A period of "unwinding" is common. "I just got lost for a couple of weeks—went on a huge binge." Then comes the effort to find a niche. They canvass the situation and begin to make their moves. Many head for school. Under the liberal Veterans Pension and Readjustment Assistance Act of 1967 they can get a month of schooling for each month of service up to 36 months. Others look for jobs—and are in great demand. Better jobs and better pay await those who can qualify. Many firms are eager to enter veterans in training programs. Racial barriers are falling rapidly. The National Urban League operates an extensive program of veterans' services, particularly in the area of job placement.[*] It receives growing support from industry. Nevertheless, civilian readjustment for the Negro veteran is often agonizing.[*]

The veteran is a boy no longer, but a man. His readjustment includes the discovery that he has crossed a divide. He cannot return to what he left behind. Home is not what it was. He is different, too, for he's done a lot of living since he went away. Things have changed. There's no going back. A large percentage of veterans do not return to their former communities, but seek a new life elsewhere.

Re-entry after Twenty Years

The veteran with perhaps the most difficult re-entry problem is the military careerist. To relocate in a highly competitive civilian economy after twenty or more years of living within a rigidly structured, paternalistic system is far from easy. An admiral-turned-stockbroker commented wryly, "I used to have two 'white-hats' outside my door keeping people out, and now I beg people to come in." The transition from a long dependency to a sudden independency can be painful. Servicemen's need for assistance in re-adjusting to civilian life has produced a number of responses.

Project Transition

One of these is known as "Project Transition." This Department of Defense program, which went into effect permanently in all services on January 6, 1968, is offered to all enlisted personnel who have from one to six months of service time remaining, and who volunteer for it. Priority is given to those who:

—are combat disabled,
—are ineligible to reenlist,

[*] Veterans Affairs Office, National Urban League, 55 E. 52nd Street, New York, New York 10022

—entered service with no civilian job experience and did not acquire a civilian-related skill during active duty,
—served almost exclusively in combat type military specialties,
—desire upgrading of military skills which are civilian-related, but which require broadening to make them usable in civilian life,
—need freshening of civilian skills acquired prior to service,
—have low educational achievement.

Many business and industrial firms participate, often on military installations. Job placement is an integral part of the program. Vocational training is provided by industry or by the Department of Labor and the Department of Health, Education, and Welfare. Other Federal Departments, such as the Post Office, are also training servicemen.

Another Response: Church Jobs for Veterans

Many veterans, particularly some who are older and who retired with government pensions, are interested in the church and would like to work for it. The church and institutions related to it need skilled personnel and, while unable to compete with the salaries available in industry, they do offer many opportunities for useful and satisfying work. Military personnel can contribute much to the church's work.

They should direct inquiries and resumes to councils of churches, denominational headquarters (national and regional), church-affiliated hospitals and schools, local churches, and the following agencies:

PROTESTANT

The General Commission on Chaplains and Armed Forces Personnel,
122 Maryland Ave., N.E.
Washington, D.C.   20002

CATHOLIC

The National Catholic Community Service
Personnel Department
1312 Massachusetts Ave., N.W.
Washington, D.C.   20005

JEWISH

National Jewish Welfare Board,
Director of Community Services,
145 E. 32nd St.,
New York, N.Y.   10016

Church leaders who seek personnel for their staffs may send inquiries to the above or to:

> The Office of the Director,
> PROJECT TRANSITION
> Office of the Assistant
> Secretary of Defense (Manpower)
> The Pentagon, Washington, D.C. 20301

The Veterans Administration

The Veterans Administration heads any listing of resources for veterans. The Congress has enacted far-reaching and liberal benefits for ex-servicemen. It is impossible to catalogue these here. A convenient summary of them may be found in a booklet called *Federal Benefits for Veterans and Dependents* (VA Fact Sheet IS-I, January, 1968, VA Information Service, available at VA offices). For all detailed information consult a local or regional office of the VA. *Do not* write the VA Central Office in Washington concerning benefits. Veterans residing in foreign countries, except the Republic of the Philippines, should contact the nearest American Embassy or Consulate.

GI life insurance is administered at the VA Center in St. Paul or Philadelphia. For any information concerning a policy, write directly to the VA center administering it, giving the insured's policy number, or else, full name, date of birth, and service number.

The Church and the Returning Serviceman

What can the churches do for those returning from military service? No collective action seems necessary. Our legislatures, Federal and State, have acted to ease the veteran's readjustment. Public machinery is functioning. The Defense Department estimates that perhaps 150,000 men a year will need the extensive vocational training offered in its PROJECT TRANSITION. Competent civilian agencies are available. There is no need for the churches to attempt to duplicate or compete. They should employ existing facilities and move into new areas of unmet need. The new veterans will in most cases return to cities or metropolitan areas and thus contribute still another facet to the already crowded urban scene which so preoccupies both nation and church.

Don't Count on His Coming to Church!

The most useful thing which church leaders can do is to alert clergymen and congregations to the presence of these veterans and to suggest the need for imaginative pastoral concern. The local church may have an opportunity to greet the returning serviceman. "May" is used advisedly, for the church cannot assume that the ex-GI will now seek it out. In fact, if through two or three years of service, the young man has received no letters, no expressions of interest from the congregation, he may respond in kind.

If no contact is kept the problem of approaching (him) after demobilization is made almost insurmountable. . . . If you have not written, no amount of concern you profess will make much difference to him. He will know that you did not care enough when he was away.[6]

Not only may a church, because of its neglect, not see its young men again; it may keep them out of all churches.

On the other hand, a church may benefit from the pastoral interest shown by persons it will never see. The veteran may come in as a stranger who remembers the Christian love shown across the miles by his home pastor and people—or by Christians in the distant land in which he served. He may return unmarried, or with a foreign-born bride and children, their own or adopted. He may be a young man who needs little help, but would appreciate a welcome. Or, he may be an older veteran who is finding readjustment to civilian ways rather difficult. In either case, pastor and people should be ready.

The task will seem more natural and perhaps a bit easier if they have already interested themselves in their own young people who face the draft. They will perceive that to aid the veteran is but a matter of following through. As they learned about Selective Service they will learn VA procedures—and will not hesitate to refer a need to the nearest source of expert assistance. Intelligent interest, affection, and respect—not expertise—are needed from civilian churchmen.

Some Suggestions

In addressing the veteran in 1968, the following suggestions, first published during World War II, still bear repeating:

- Treat him as an essentially normal, upstanding, competent person, not as an invalid . . .
- Let him talk—or keep silent—about his experiences . . .
- If he is injured, treat him naturally as you always have . . .
- Create an atmosphere of expectancy: encourage him to take up his favorite hobby or sport, to go back to work as soon as he is able, and to lead a normal social life, but avoid pushing or regulating him . . .

- Give him time . . .
- Help and reassure him about his religious development . . .
- Get professional help if need be. Don't just muddle through . . .
- Let your own faith and beauty of spirit be your chief assets . . .
- Above all, be a good listener . . .
- And remember—he is not first an ex-service man, he is first a person, a human being, a child of God. He is not a problem, but like other people he has problems, and we may help him solve them . . .
- Remember, he has not shared your experiences . . .
- Expect him to be different in some ways . . .
- Take time to get acquainted again and to find ways of getting along together . . .
- Be non-shockable about his new slants on life . . .
- Be friendly, even warm, but not over-cheery . . .[7]

In these various ways pastors and lay people can contribute more than they realize to a veteran's readjustment. He may never tell them. Yet, as he resumes his place beside them, both he and they may possibly appreciate more strongly the assertion with which this book began: from its beginning to its ending the Armed Forces Ministry belongs to civilians.

NOTES AND BIBLIOGRAPHY

1. *This U.S.A.* by Ben J. Wattenberg, N.Y. Pocket Books, Inc., 1967 pp. 218-20, paper, 95¢, 386 pp.
2. *Ibid.* p. 219.
3. *The Church and Demobilization* by J. Gordon Chamberlin, N.Y. Abingdon-Cokesbury, 1945, p. 29. cloth, $1.00, 117 pp.
4. cf. *The Re-entry Problem of the Vietvets* by William B. Furlong, NEW YORK TIMES MAGAZINE, 7 May, 1967, p. 23.
5. cf. *When the Black G.I. Comes Back from Vietnam* by Sol Stern, NEW YORK TIMES MAGAZINE, 24 March, 1968, pp. 27.
6. Chamberlin, *op. cit.* p. 83.
7. *Ibid.* pp. 84-5.
   cf. *Sequels to a Military Career: the Retired Military Professional* by Albert D. Biderman in *The New Military* edited by Morris Janowitz, pp. 287-336, Russell Sage Foundation, N.Y., 1964.
   Soldier to Civilian by George K. Pratt, N.Y. McGraw-Hill, 1944.
   The Veteran Comes Back by Willard Waller, N.Y. Dryden Press, 1944.

Bibliography

SOURCES OF MATERIALS

The General Commission on Chaplains and Armed Forces Personnel, 122 Maryland Ave., N.E. Washington, D.C. 20002.

Publishes numerous pamphlets and small books about military service, some of which are listed below. Also publishes *The Link,* a Protestant monthly magazine for Armed Forces Personnel; and *The Chaplain,* published bi-monthly.

"Meet Your New Pastor—the Chaplain." Introducing the chaplain and his ministry.

"Stay on That High Road." Appeal to travel the road of high ideals.

"Your Church Back Home." Letter from home pastor to Johnny.

"Say a Good Word." Plea for Christian witness and evangelism.

"How to Worship in a Strange Congregation." Help for worshipers constantly on the move.

"You Don't Have to Drink." Convincing evidence that you really don't.

"The Struggle for the World." A penetrating analysis of the struggle between Communism and Christianity for the world.

"Peace Is My Profession." Peace is the world's need and the serviceman's profession.

"Say There, Serviceman!" A challenge to Christlike living during the military years.

"As the Twig Is Bent." Four factors in a young man's life back home are keys to the kind of soldier he will become.

"Urgent Need to Develop the Laity." Making the church relevant to the world is a task for laymen; suggestions to chaplains on how to develop the lay ministry.

"Protestants Believe." Brief statement of our basic beliefs.

"Correspondence Courses on Religion." Listing of correspondence courses on religion available through colleges and denominations.

"The New Life." How to Become a Christian.

"Christians Stand Guard." Counsel to the new recruit going into military service.

"Chaplain Service in Veterans Administration Hospitals." The magnificent ministry of VA chaplains.

Ministry to Armed Forces by Edward I. Swanson. A guide for clergymen, counselors, and congregations who minister to those in or entering the Armed Forces.

"Approach to Marriage." Discussion of pre-marital sex relations; love; the girl you marry; forces threatening the home, etc.

"Sex, Love, Marriage and the Home." What Is Love? A Date or a Mate? A Christian View of Sex, etc.

"I Will Look Up." Devotional booklet for hospital use.

"A Book of Prayers for the Armed Forces."

"Who We Are" by Stanley I. Stuber. Protestants: Their origin, their thrilling history, their beliefs, their place in the world scene today.

"Scripture Calendar: The Lord's Prayer." Wallet-size calendar containing on one side "The Lord's Prayer"; on the other the yearly calendar with some dates to remember.

"Scripture Calendar: The Ten Commandments." Wallet-size calendar containing on one side the Ten Commandments; on the other the yearly calendar with some dates to remember.

The American Baptist Convention, Committee on Chaplains, Valley Forge, Pa.   19481

Publishes tracts for servicemen.

The Christian Reformed Church in the United States and Canada. The Young Calvinist Federation, 2365 Nelson Ave., S.E., Grand Rapids, Michigan   49507.

"Get Ready!" A 29-page booklet for young men entering service.

Christian Science—Christian Science Activities for the Armed Services, 107 Falmouth St., Boston, Massachusetts   02115.

"Information for Christian Scientists Serving in the Armed Forces."

"A Healing Ministry." Christian Science Activities for the Armed Forces, plus a film strip by this title with a recording.

Disciples of Christ, Committee on Military and Veterans Services, 222 South Downey Ave., Indianapolis, Indiana   46207.

Publishes pamphlets.

Lutheran Council, U.S.A., Division of Service to Military Personnel, 2633 16th St., N.W. Washington, D.C.   20009.

Publishes or distributes materials for servicemen on behalf of all Lutheran churches.

"Hey, There! Your Church Cares!"—leaflet (Mo. Synod)

Book: *Letters to John* by Chaplain Theodore Kleinhans. To a young man about life, love, war and other things.

"On Active Duty" by Pastor Roy G. Gesch.

National Association of Evangelicals, 1405 G. St., N.W., Washington, D.C. 20005.

Publishes a booklet, *Opportunity of a Life-Time*.

Presbyterian Church, US, Board of Christian Education, 801 E. Main St., Box 1176, Richmond, Va. 23209.

Publishes materials for young people on vocations and military service. "For Adults Only." A study guide for grade 12.

Protestant Episcopal Church, Office of the Bishop for the Armed Forces, 815 Second Ave., N.Y., N.Y. 10017.

Publishes a "Prayer Book for the Armed Forces," other tracts on military service, and distributes a Service Cross.

The Roman Catholic Church—National Catholic Community Service, Member Agency of USO, 1312 Massachusetts Ave., N.W. Washington, D.C. 20005.

Publishes materials for Catholic servicemen. Series on Serving a Great Country: (1) "The Serviceman—Adjusting to the New Life," (2) "The Serviceman and the Military Capital Sin"; (3) The Serviceman and Sex"; (4) "The Serviceman and Marriage"; (5) "The Serviceman and Spiritual Resources"; (6) "The Serviceman—Patriotism and Morale."

"The Catholic Family in Uniform"; "Man Your Battle Stations"; "Fall In!" "Greetings! For Young Men about to enter Military Service" (Sept. 1952); "Guide to Greetings!"

Tracts: "Do You Want to Live Forever?"; "A Word on the Word"; "Drink—All You Want"; "Get on the Beam"; "We Live in a Blasphemous Age"; "What is the Catholic Church?—A Building or a Body?"

The Salvation Army, 120-130 W. 14th St., New York, N.Y. 10011.

Publishes devotional booklet and other materials.

Seventh-Day Adventist, National Service Organization, 6840 Eastern Ave., N.W. Washington, D.C. 20012.

Publishes many leaflets for servicemen.

Southern Baptist Convention, Division of Chaplaincy, Home Mission Board, 161 Spring St., N.W. Atlanta, Ga. 30303.

Publishes many tracts for servicemen.

United Church of Christ, Councils for Church and Ministry and for Christian Social Action, 289 Park Ave., S., N.Y., N.Y. 10010.

Tracts on the draft and on military service.

The United Methodist Church, Commission on Chaplains, 3900 Wisconsin Ave., N.W. Washington, D.C. 20016.

Publishes tracts.

United Presbyterian Church, USA, Department of Chaplains and Service Personnel, 4125 Nebraska Ave., N.W. Washington, D.C. 20016.

Publishes tracts for servicemen. Distributes a Celtic Cross Medallion.

The Y.M.C.A., Armed Services Department, National Board of YMCA's, 291 Broadway, N.Y., N.Y. 10007.

Publishes material on pre-military counseling; operates Y units for Armed Forces personnel.
"20 Questions: The YMCA in the USO 1861-1961: 100 Years of YMCA Service to America's Armed Forces."

The Y.W.C.A., USO Division, National Board, YWCA, 600 Lexington Ave., New York, N.Y. 10022.

Publishes a leaflet: "The YWCA in USO."

SOURCES OF FILMS
Army Films

The films listed below may be borrowed without charge from the Army Film and Equipment Exchange serving your area. This is a selection of films; some of them are old, but still of interest. Many others, particularly more recent ones, are available. As usual with any audio-visual materials, it would be well to pre-view the film before using it to determine its usefulness. Catalogues will be sent on request.

To borrow a film for public showing write to the proper Army center for your region, as follows:

All of New England, New York, New Jersey, Pennsylvania, Maryland, Virginia, Ohio, West Virginia, Kentucky, and Delaware:
  Attn: Signal Officer
  Commanding General
  First Army
  Fort George G. Meade, Maryland   20755

North Carolina, South Carolina, Georgia, Florida, Alabama, Tennessee and Mississippi:
  Attn: Signal Officer
  Commanding General
  Third Army
  Fort McPherson, Georgia   30330

Arkansas. Texas, Oklahoma, New Mexico, Louisiana:
  Attn: Signal Officer
  Commanding General
  Fourth Army
  Fort Sam Houston, Texas   78234

Indiana, Illinois, Michigan, Wisconsin, Missouri, Kansas, Iowa, Nebraska, Minnesota, North Dakota, South Dakota, Wyoming, Colorado:
  Attn: Signal Officer
  Commanding General
  Fifth Army
  Fort Sheridan, Illinois   60038

Washington, Oregon, Idaho, Montana, Utah, Arizona, California, Alaska, and Hawaii:
  Attn: Signal Officer
  Commanding General
  Sixth Army
  Presidio, California   94129

District of Columbia:
  Commanding General
  Military District of Washington
  Washington, D.C.   20315

*AFIF 90. "The Code—The US Fighting Man's Code of Conduct." 29 min. Precepts of the 6 articles of the code; vignettes of each, with theme on surrender, capture, escape and conduct as a prisoner of war.

*AFIF 93. "Keep on Learning." 15 min. Describes the Armed Forces Education Program, what it offers, how it is organized and implemented, and how it benefits the serviceman.

*AFIF 99. "Old Glory." 28 min. Evolution of the American flag from 1607 when the English Flag flew over Jamestown, till 1960 when the new 50 star flag became a reality.

*AFIF 128. "The Vote." 11 min. Origin of absentee voting system. How eligible military personnel and their dependents can cast their votes in the forthcoming elections.

*AFIF 153. "The Unique War." 25 min. This is the story of the fighting man and his unit in Vietnam—whether Soldier—Sailor—Marine—or Airman, defending against aggression.

*AFMR 620. "Men with Wings." 14 min. Reports on the fifty years of military aviation ranging from the first flights of the Wright Brothers at Fort Myer to the modern supersonic jets of today's armaments.

*AFMR 649. "Service Academies." 19 min. This film inculcates a deeper appreciation of the service academies, an understanding of admission procedures, and a fuller realization of the professional competence, leadership abilities and balanced development that the academies foster in the cadets and midshipmen they graduate into the officer ranks.

*MF 20-8322. "Time To Go." 28 min. Organization, purpose and operation of selective service system. Personnel and activities of local boards. Requirements, obligations, classification and deferments of draftees. Pre-induction processing, induction and benefits of Army training.

MF 20-8668. "Traditions and Achievements of the Army." 26 min. Reviews the role of the Army throughout the history of the Nation. Emphasizes the role of the modern soldier.

*MY 35-7858. "No Greater Heritage." 21 min. Morale and the fine heritage of the Women's Army Corps.

*MF 45-8288. "Adjustment to Military Life." 18 min. Adjustments a trainee is required to make in his transition from civilian to military life. Emphasis on physical and moral standards.

118

*MF 45-8438. "Letter From a Mother." 10 min. Report of an American Mother's feelings showing not only her deep affection for her son but an understanding of the role he must play in the defense of his country.

*MF 45-8440. "The Soldier's Mission and Responsibilities." 13 min. Depicts the soldier's mission and responsibilities in the defense of his country.

*MF 45-8521. "The Making of a West Pointer." 40 min. Origin and mission of the US Military Academy, its traditions and ceremonies. Comprehensive view of life of cadet from time of entry to graduation, his course of study and recreation activities.

*MF 45-8652. "A Look at Your Army." 12 min. A message from General Maxwell D. Taylor, Army Chief of Staff, on the vital role of the Army and the merits of an Army Career.

*TF 16-3202. "The Chaplain and the Commander." 29 min. Explains the role of the Chaplain in the military service and shows how he assists the commander in the fulfillment of the military objective.

* Cleared for Television

Navy Films
All requests for the loan of Navy motion pictures should be sent to the Commandant of the Naval District in which your city is located, addressed to the Navy Public Affairs Office. The nearest Navy Recruiting Office can tell you the number of the Naval District you are in.

To assure the best service, please include the title and Navy serial number of the requested film, date desired, and any alternate dates.

Each District publishes a film catalogue which is normally available upon request. Here are the addresses of the naval districts.

First Naval District
495 Summer Street
Boston, Mass. 02110

Fifth Naval District
US Naval Base
Norfolk, Va. 23511

Third Naval District
90 Church Street
New York, N.Y. 10007

Sixth Naval District
US Naval Base
Charleston, S.C. 29508

Fourth Naval District
US Naval Base
Philadelphia, Pa. 19112

Eighth Naval District
US Naval Station
New Orleans, La. 70140

Ninth Naval District
US Naval Training Center
Great Lakes, Ill. 60088

Twelfth Naval District
Federal Office Bldg.
San Francisco, Calif. 94102

Eleventh Naval District
937 North Harbor Drive
San Diego, Calif. 92130

Thirteenth Naval District
US Naval Air Station
Seattle, Washington 98115

Potomac River Naval Command
US Naval Gun Factory
Washington, D.C. 20390

*MN-10063. "Careers in Oceanography." 28 min. Color. 1965. The film presents the challenge and adventure of oceanography and its vital importance to defense and the economy.

*MN-10068. "Campus to Command." 28 min. Color. 1965. From the use of a mariner's traditional tools to understanding the evolution of complex weapons systems, the academic schedule of three candidates at Officer Candidate School is followed against a background of Naval tradition. The experience of command is illustrated by the graduates' duties on a destroyer, on a LST and in the service forces.

*10278D. "The Corpsman." 14 min. Color. 1966. The battlefield call for help, "corpsman," is traced through the jungles of Vietnam. A marine corporal is wounded and the response of the corpsman is traced from evacuation by helicopter to the operating table, the ward and home. The reasons behind the lowest mortality rate amongst the wounded in Vietnam of the wars in which America has fought is documented.

*MH-10278G. "For Thou Art With Me." 14 min. Color. 1967. The quiet, essential role of the Chaplain is described in meeting the needs of Marines in a combat situation in Vietnam. The part of the Chaplain in aiding the people of Vietnam is also featured.

*MN-9400B. "Man and the FBM." 28 min. Color. 1960. Before reporting to fleet ballistic missile submarines, qualified submariners must undergo eighteen months intensive, specialized training. This film shows men in training at New London, Connecticut, the Guided Missile School in Dam Neck, Virginia, and on board the floating laboratory vessel USS Observation Island. Two FBMs are shown briefly.

*MC-9489. "Mail Call." 13½ min. B/W. 1960. In this joint production of the Post Office and Navy Department, Postmaster General Arthur E. Summerfield and Admiral Arleigh A. Burke discuss the importance of mail to Americans overseas. A small girl mails a letter to her father. The letter is followed through the Postal Concentration Center, to Rome by commercial plane, then to a Navy plane and finally a carrier operating in the Mediterranean.

*MN-7339. "Navy Nurse." 22 min. Color. 1952. As Ensign Janet Lee packs to report to her second Navy duty station, her thoughts flash back to her indoctrination. After a panorama of Navy medical services, the film concentrates on the working and teaching relationships Ensign Lee builds with the four corpsmen working with her.

Air Force Films

The following are available from the USAF Library Center, 8900 South Broadway, St. Louis, Mo. 63125. Many may be obtained at Air Force installations near you. Consult the nearest Air Force Recruiting station for the best source. The USAF Film Library Center publishes a catalogue.

Clearance Code: TH—Theatrical
PS—Public Service
PE—Public Exhibition
AF—Air Force Film (producer)
DOD—Dept. of Defense film

SFP 1210. "Decision for Leadership." 23 min. Color. 1964. PE, TV, PS. Portrays the USAF Officer's Training School. Depicts career opportunities offered qualified college graduates. Shows training, scope of curriculum, and physical training program.

SFP 1211. "Letter From an Airman." 17 min. Color. 1964. AF, PE, TV, TH, PS. Portrays an airman's thoughts as he writes his brother about Air Force basic training. Depicts trainee life from induction to special assignment. Cites the specialized training that prepares the airman for a rewarding career, promotion and opportunity to serve the Air Force with purpose and pride.

SFP 1234. "Growth into Leadership at the United States Air Force Academy." 22 min. Color. 1965. AF, PE, TV, TH, PS. Describes full scope of Air Force Academy leadership training program. Shows use of conference and problem situations to develop student potential and versatility. Reviews exciting and rewarding career opportunities for academy graduates.

SFP 1235. "Stars in Their Eyes." 15 min. Color. 1963. Comm. PS, TV, TH.

This film is tailored to the space-minded lad who envisions his future in the stars. Points out the long, narrow road, filled with study, work and physical training, that lies between him and the exacting career of an astronaut. Tours the Aerospace Research Pilot School where trainees are carefully fitted with the physical, mental, and psychological attributes needed to survive outer space environment.

SFP 1240. "From Kitty Hawk to Aerospace." 21 min. Color. 1965. AF, PE, TV. Traces history of American aviation. Stresses influence of science and technology on advancement of aircraft. Highlights milestones that mark the road from primitive bi-wing machines to supersonic aircraft and space vehicles. Interviews Generals James Doolittle, Benjamin Foulois, and Bernard Schriever who present their views on the significance of aerospace power.

SFP 1064. "Counselor in Uniform." 20 min. B/W. 1961. AF, PE, TV, TH, PS. Portrays role of the Air Force Judge Advocate in protecting the constitutional and statutory rights of AF personnel in the States and abroad; in providing legal assistance and counseling services for personnel involved in criminal lawsuits; and in protecting Air Force interests in matters of contracts, patents, copyrights, etc.

SFP 1073. "Prepare the Man." 25 min. Color. 1962. AF, PE, TV, TH, PS. Explains new concepts in selective recruiting, proper replacement, and highly specialized training of personnel. Points out continuing need for missile crews, pilots, electronic specialists, scientists, and related high level personnel.

SFP 1323. "Mats Worldwide Mission." 38 min. Color. 1965. AF, PE, TV, TH, PS. Reviews missions, organization and facilities. On site scenes present command's capability to airlift food, medicine and aid to disaster areas and to transport troops and equipment for military maneuvers and international crises.

SFP 1355. "A Hitch in Time." 6 min. Color. 1964. AF. Points out advantages of an Air Force career. Compares military and civilian life in terms of pay, education, retirement and fringe benefits.

SFP 1495. "The Man in the Blue Suit." 14 min. Color. 1965. AF. Portrays Air Force life as a profession comparable to teaching, medicine, law and the clergy in terms of motivation, required skills, ethics and commitments.

SFP 1320. "Profile of the Future." 14½ min. Color. 1964. AF. Cites important role of young officers in many key phases of space age work at Cape

Kennedy. Depicts opportunities in these careers for college graduates.

Coast Guard Films

These and other films may be obtained from the following Coast Guard Offices; a film catalogue is also available:

COMMANDER
1st Coast Guard District
1400 Customhouse, Boston, Mass.   02109

2d Coast Guard District
Federal Building, 1520 Market Street, St. Louis, Mo.   63103

3d Coast Guard District
Customhouse, New York, N.Y.   10004

5th Coast Guard District
Federal Building, 431 Crawford Street, Portsmouth, Va.   23705

7th Coast Guard District
Room 1203, Federal Building, 51 Southwest First Avenue, Miami, Florida   33130

8th Coast Guard District
Customhouse, New Orleans, La.   70130

9th Coast Guard District
Main Post Office Bldg, W. Third and Prospect Sts., Cleveland, Ohio   44113

11th Coast Guard District
Heartwell Bldg., 19 Pine Avenue, Long Beach, Calif.   90802

12th Coast Guard District
630 Sansome Street, San Francisco, Calif.   94501

13th Coast Guard District
618 Second Avenue, Seattle, Wash.   98104

14th Coast Guard District
1347 Kapiolani Boulevard, Honolulu, Hawaii   96814

17th Coast Guard District
Post Office Box 2631, Juneau, Alaska   99801

And
Commandant (CPI), US Coast Guard
1300 E Street, N.W., Washington, D.C.   20226

"United States Coast Guard." 16 mm. 28 min. Color. 1958. Presents an overall view of Coast Guard operations, from the 1790 origin to the present time. The active peacetime service is shown in the multiplicity of its duties, including port-security, maintenance of aids-to-navigation, promotion, and enforcement of maritime safety measures, ice and weather patrol, search and rescue operations, small boat safety. The Coast Guard Academy and receiving stations are also shown. A swiftly-paced resume of this many-faceted service, with an introduction by the Commandant. Supersedes 1948 film. Cleared for Television.

"Coast Guard Cutters Around the Continent." 16 mm. 28 min. Color. 1958. This documentary film presents the story of the Coast Guard participation in the 1957 Arctic operations, including circumnavigation of North America. US Coast Guard Cutters Stories, Bramble, and Spar are shown in their sometimes uncertain but eventually successful battle to locate and chart the last link in the 450-year search for the famous "Northwest Passage." Winner of the following film awards: International Film Festival, Edinburgh; Canadian Film Festival, Ottawa; and International Film Festival, Salerno.

"Coast Guard Icebreakers." 16 mm. 28 min. Color. 1958. In striking color, this film provides a panoramic view of the Coast Guard's far-flung ice-breaking operations in the Arctic and Antarctic, and on the Great Lakes and rivers. It includes participation in the construction of the Thule Air Base in Greenland, and historical sequences showing the development of the icebreaking function. Cleared for Television.

"Salute to the Coast Guard." 16 mm. 28 min. B/W. 1964. One of the US Army's THE BIG PICTURE television series, this is their tribute to a service that has logged a long and distinguished record in the annals of the sea. Produced by the Army Pictorial Center from Coast Guard stock footage, except for a few scenes at the start of the film, shot at APC. Presents the roles and missions of the Coast Guard from its origin in 1790. Narrated by Alex Drier, swiftly paced.

Marine Corps Films (Obtainable through nearest Marine Corps Recruiting Office)

MH 9438. "Bright Future." 14½ min. Color. 1961. This is a Woman Marine Officer-procurement film showing the executive-type billets available to young women in the Marine Corps Officer Program.

MH 10140. "Educational Opportunities in the Marine Corps." 14 min. Color. 1966. How educational opportunities are related to military duties and future employment, and how they benefit the individual Marine in the Corps and in civilian life.

MH 10382. "A Day in Vietnam." 28 min. Color. 1967. Depicts various facets of war in Vietnam. Especially directed towards civilian viewing. Narrated by Jack Webb.

MC 10447. "Hovering Angel." 10 min. Color. 1967. Examples of helicopter rescue operations. Produced by Boeing Vertol Company.

MH 10278B. "The Full Blade." 14 min. Color. 1965. Depicts a portion of the Civic Action program being carried out by the Marines in Vietnam. Includes scenes depicting food distribution and the rendering of medical assistance to the Vietnamese people.

Films on Conscientious Objection

All films noted below are controversial in nature. They seek to raise questions and to stir up reactions. They should only be used as stimulators when there is a context for listening and for offering help with the questions that will inevitably follow a viewing.

"Vietnam: Journal of War," a 52 min. black and white, 16 mm film, produced by the British Broadcasting Co., rents for $25 from Peter M. Robeck Co., 230 Park Ave., New York City   10017.

"Inside North Vietnam," by Felix Greene, a 1½ hour, 16 mm color film, rents for $150 from Rogosin Films, 144 Bleeker St., New York City   10012.

"Vietnam: How Did We Get In? How Can We Get Out?," by David Schoenbrun, a 33 minute, 16mm film rents for $50 from American Documentary Films, Inc., 379 Bay St., San Francisco or 144 Bleeker St., New York City.

"Alternatives." 24 min. Color. Study Guide. Produced by National Service Board for Religious Objectors and cooperating agencies, 1959. Available from the Audio-Visual Film Library (815 Second Ave., New York   10017) and from the Fellowship of Reconciliation (N. Broadway, Upper Nyack, N.Y.). Rental $3.50. Available also from Cokesbury Bookstores (six regional centers and many outlets throughout the country). Rental $7.50. The film deals with noncombatant service (I-AO), civilian services (I-O), and nonregistration, devoting major time and attention to the latter pair. It presents the legitimate alternatives to military service afforded under the draft law.

INDEX